AWESOME EXPERIMENTS

ARCTURUS

This edition published in 2011 by Arcturus Publishing Limited
26/27 Bickels Yard, 151–153 Bermondsey Street,
London SE1 3HA

Editors: Alex Woolf and Joe Harris
Design and photography: Sally Henry and Trevor Cook
Cover design: Peter Ridley
Consultant: Keith Clayson
Picture credits: Sally Henry and Trevor Cook

ISBN: 978-1-84837-604-5
CH001550US

Printed in Singapore

Supplier 06, Date 0611, Print run 1010

MESSAGE TO PARENTS
Please note that the experiments in this book are intended to be undertaken
with adult supervision. The components and apparatus in the experiments
should not be used in ways other than those instructed. The publisher accepts
no liability for any damage or injury arising out of or in connection with the
publication of this title.

AWESOME EXPERIMENTS

Trevor Cook

ARCTURUS

Contents

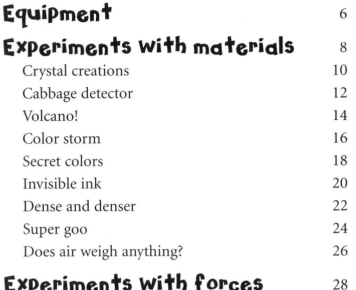

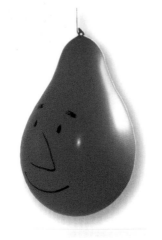

Equipment

You should easily find many things that you need for our experiments around the home.

20 minutes

This tells you about how long a project could take.

This symbol means you might need adult help.

Kitchen equipment Ask before borrowing saucepans, plates, baking sheets, funnels, and anything else from the kitchen.

Freezer Always ask permission if you need to use the freezer. Perhaps an adult can clear a space or a drawer for you to use.

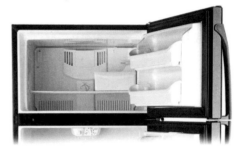

Tea kettle You will sometimes need to use boiling water. Ask an adult to help. Check that the kettle is turned off when you have finished with it.

Food ingredients Be careful when using food ingredients or anything from unmarked bottles. Check with an adult and get permission first.

Matches Always take great care with matches. Ask an adult to help you. Extra long or kitchen matches would be very useful in some of our experiments.

Food dye is used for coloring cakes and sweets. It's very strong. You will only need a few drops. Try to avoid getting dye on yourself or your clothes!

Oven glove Always use padded gloves if you are handling anything hot. Avoid painful burns!

Glue Glue stick is best for fixing paper to paper or paper to card. Universal glue is a rubbery stuff that sticks most things to most other things!

Candles and tea lights Be sure to handle with care. Never leave lighted candles or tea lights unattended.

Scissors Use safe scissors with round tips for your science experiments. Keep them away from young children.

Wire We use several kinds of wire in our experiments. In the ones about electricity and magnetism, the kind of wire found inside flexible power cords is ideal. Ask an adult to help you remove the outer covering from the cord and strip the colored insulation from the ends of the wires you find inside. For experiments such as the balancing act on page 32, we need a thin, flexible wire. We've used the sort made for tying up garden plants.

Wire stripper In the electrical experiments you'll need to have the metal conductor exposed at the end of the wires. This hand tool is used to remove insulation. You might have one in your household toolkit. Get an adult to help you do this!

Batteries We've used a size that's called AA. It's a very common size and you'll find them used in lots of things around the home.

Hammer Most homes have a hammer somewhere. Take care when you use it and put it away when you've finished!

Experiments with materials

Everything around us—and inside us—is made of materials. Our bodies are made up mostly of carbon, hydrogen, oxygen, nitrogen, calcium, and phosphorus.

Carbon is the fourth most common element in the universe. It is found in the form of diamonds, charcoal, and pencil "lead," which is really graphite.

This symbol is a corrosive chemical warning.

Hydrogen is the most common element. With oxygen, it forms water as well as corrosive (destructive) chemicals.

Oxygen is used in welding.

Oxygen is the third most common element and makes up 21 percent of air.

In May 1937, a famous German airship, the Hindenburg, burst into flames near its mooring mast in New Jersey, USA. Hydrogen and oxygen made an explosive mixture.

78 percent of air is nitrogen. It's a gas that helps to make rocket fuel, explosives, and fertilizer.

We have calcium in our teeth and bones. It is a metal also found in cement and in fireworks.

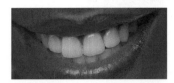

Phosphorus is a metal that self-combusts (lights on fire) when exposed to air.

It's used in making fertilizers and matches.

Crystal creations

less than 1 hour

A crystal is a solid material which forms itself into a very regular three-dimensional pattern. Crystals are formed when a liquid cools and turns into a solid. The arrangement of *atoms* in the solid produces the shape of the crystal. An example of this is when water is cooled and becomes ice.

You will need:
- sugar, glass jar
- coarse string, a popsicle stick
- hot water, spoon
- salt, sand, soil
- 2 glass jars, plastic bag
- paper coffee filter or paper towels
- funnel and a small plate

The plan
We are going to dissolve some substances in water. We will try to grow crystals. Then we will use crystallization to purify salt.

Experiment 1

water level

end of string

Put some hot water into a jam jar. Water from the hot faucet should be hot enough.

Add sugar, one spoon at a time, using the popsicle stick as a stirrer. Keep adding more sugar until you can't dissolve any more. You will see undissolved sugar left at the bottom of the jar.

Tie the string to the popsicle stick, hang it in the sugar solution, and let cool. The string is a good surface for growing crystals.

4 As the solution cools, crystals begin to form on the string. Be patient, it can take a few days for crystals to form, provided you have made a saturated solution.

What else can you do?

Try different kinds of sugar! Light brown, dark brown, superfine—check in your kitchen cabinet.

What's going on?

The sugar dissolves in water to form a sugar solution. Hot water allows more sugar to dissolve. As the water cools it cannot hold as much sugar in solution, and some sugar changes back to a solid.

Experiment 2

1 Mix salt, soil, and sand together thoroughly with a spoon, on a piece of plastic bag.

2 Stir the mixture into warm water and let settle overnight.

3 Pour the liquid through a paper filter, taking care to leave the sediment in the bottom of the jar. Leave the filtered liquid on the plate in a warm place.

What's going on?

Only the salt dissolves in the water. The heavier particles of sand and soil sink to the bottom of the jar. Filtering removes the smaller sand and soil particles. Finally, on the plate, the water *evaporates* to leave just the salt crystals.

Cabbage detector

You can use cabbage water to tell whether liquids are acids, *neutral,* or *alkaline.* Examples of acids are acetic acid (in vinegar) and citric acid (in oranges and lemons). Strong acids can eat away metal. A very strong *alkali* can cause chemical burns.

You will need:

- knife for chopping, 2 glasses
- heat-resistant bowls or jars, tea kettle
- white vinegar • baking soda
- plastic dropper • water
- red cabbage

The plan

We are going to make an indicator that will tell us which liquids are acids and which are alkalis.

What to do:

1 Ask an adult to chop about two cupfuls of cabbage into small pieces. Place them in the bowl.

2 Pour some boiling water into a bowl of red cabbage and leave for 15 minutes. Ask an adult to pour the kettle.

3 Pour off the liquid into a bowl. This liquid is our "indicator."

4 You need two known liquids to test your indicator. We are using white vinegar (acid) and a solution of baking soda in water (alkali).

5 Add indicator to your solution in drops. Watch the indicator color change. Wash the glasses thoroughly between tests.

6 See where the results fall on this chart.

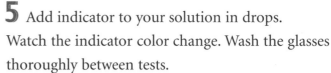

more acidic		neutral		more alkaline	
red	purple	blue-violet	blue-green	green-yellow	

What's going on?

The *pigments* from the cabbage react with acids and alkalis to change the color. The juice should turn pink in acidic solutions and green in alkaline ones. Put some indicator drops in plain water. This is your neutral color. Use your indicator to test other liquids and compare the results.

What else can you do?

Try other kinds of colored vegetable juice to see if they make indicators.

Jargon Buster
Acids are found in citrus fruits.
Alkalis are found in soap.

Volcano!

about 2 hours

We are going to take another look at acids and alkalis. When we mix the two we can get the effect of a *volcano*! Get some friends to help!

You will need:
- flour, salt, cooking oil
- tablespoon, 2 old baking sheets
- large bowl, funnel, small plastic bottle
- red food coloring, mixing jug
- dishwashing liquid, baking soda
- warm water, vinegar
- black paint, paintbrush, glitter

The plan
We are going to show what happens when an acid is mixed with an alkali.

What to do:

1 For salt dough, mix together 6 cups of flour, 2 cups of salt, 4 tablespoons of cooking oil and 1½ cups of water in a large bowl. Work all the ingredients together until smooth and firm.

2 Stand the bottle on the baking sheet. Mould the salt dough around the base of the bottle.

3 Build the dough up into a cone shape. Cover the bottle right up to the top, but don't let any dough fall in. When dry, roughly paint the cone black. Add some glitter.

4 Mix 10 drops of red food coloring with warm water. Pour 1¾ cups into the bottle.

5 Put 8 drops of dishwashing liquid into the bottle.

6 Add 3 tablespoons of baking soda, to create "lava."

7 Pour in vinegar to fill the bottle, and remove the funnel. Stand well back!

8 Watch the foaming "lava" as it pours down the volcano! Take care not to get any food color on your clothes!

What's going on?

The vinegar is an acid. The baking soda is an alkali. They react together violently producing (among other things) carbon dioxide gas. As gases take up more space than solids and liquids, the mixture bubbles up and out of the bottle.

Warning!

Do not try mixing other household chemicals unless you are sure it is safe to do so! Ask an adult.

What else can you do?

Try putting the red cabbage indicator from page 10 into white vinegar and then add baking soda, a little at a time. What do you think will happen to the indicator?

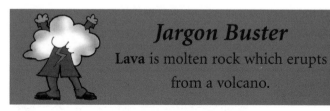

Jargon Buster
Lava is molten rock which erupts from a volcano.

15

Color storm

45 minutes

Oil and water don't mix. Or do they? In fact milk contains both. Here's how you use oil and water to make a whirling pattern.

You will need:

- 2 white plates or saucers
- whole milk
- dishwashing liquid
- matchstick or skewer
- 3 or 4 colors of food coloring
- notebook and pencil

The plan

We are going to add food coloring to water and then to milk. Then we'll see what happens when we drop dishwashing liquid into the mixtures.

What to do:

1 Pour water into a saucer or plate. Wait for a minute or until the water stops moving.

2 Put some evenly spaced drops of food coloring in the water.

3 Pour some milk into the other saucer or plate. Wait for a minute for the milk to stop moving.

4 Put some drops of food coloring in the milk, evenly spaced.

5 Add one drop of dishwashing liquid to each of the saucers.

6 Look at your saucers after a few minutes, then again after 10 minutes.

7 Look at your saucers again after 20 minutes. Use a notepad and pencil to write down the results.

Make notes of what you see:

- What happens when you add the food coloring to the water?
- What happens when you add the coloring to the milk?
- What happens when you add the dishwashing liquid to the water and milk?
- Read on to find out why.

What's going on?

Milk is a special mixture of fat and water called an emulsion. The fat is not dissolved in the water, but the two are mixed together (cream at the top of milk is some of the fat which has separated).

The food coloring doesn't travel through milk as readily as it does through water because it mixes with only the watery part of the milk.

When you add dishwashing liquid, two things happen—the surface tension of the water is destroyed, and the fat and water start to mix together because the dishwashing liquid breaks up the fat.

The movement of the food coloring shows you what's happening. It moves to the side of the saucer when the surface tension is broken, and it swirls in patterns as the fat and water mix together.

What else can you do?

Try other different liquids, or liquids at different temperatures. What do you think will happen?

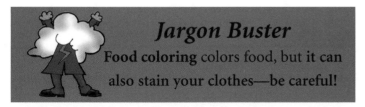

Jargon Buster
Food coloring colors food, but it can also stain your clothes—be careful!

Secret colors

25 minutes

Chromatography is a technique for separating and identifying the parts that make up a mixture.

The plan

We are going to use one type of chromatography, called paper chromatography, to find out what pigments make up different colored inks.

You will need:

- colored marker pens (not permanent or waterproof)
- blotting paper
- ruler, scissors
- tape, bowl, water
- pencil, notebook

What to do:

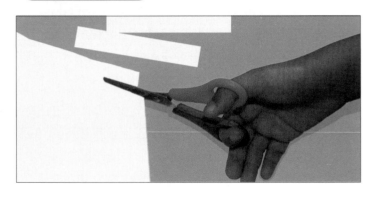

1 Cut blotting paper into 6 strips measuring 6 inches x ½ inch.

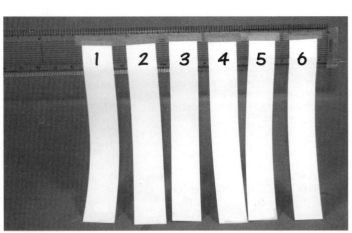

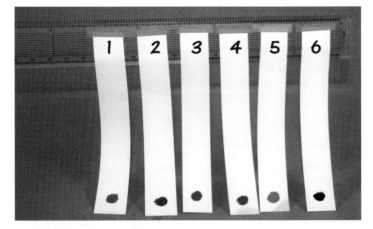

2 Number the strips and tape them to the ruler.

3 Put a small dot of a different color on each strip, noting each strip number as the color is put on.

4 Fill the bowl half full with water. Hang the strips over the edge of the bowl, so that the ends are just touching the water.

5 Wait until the water is ¾ inch or so from the ruler, then remove the strips from the bowl and record the colors you see. Sometimes a black will give a very surprising result!

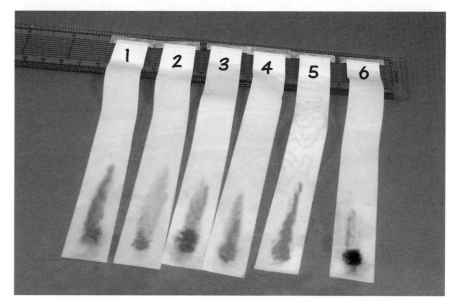

What's going on?

Water moves up the strips by capillary action and carries the pigments with it. Some pigments are more strongly attracted to the paper fibers and so are not carried so far. A color may be made of many different pigments.

What else can you do?

Try using other colored substances, for example food dye.

Jargon Buster
Capillary action is the way a liquid such as water is drawn into tiny spaces in a material by the attraction between molecules.

Invisible ink

25 minutes

It's easy to send secret messages to your friends when you write them in top secret invisible ink. The "secret" is in the combination of lemon juice and heat from a light bulb or an iron. The heat causes a chemical change in the lemon juice and makes it appear darker on paper.

The plan

It can be a little tricky to write with the 'ink'—it's invisible, after all—but once you get the hang of it, it's a fun way to share secrets with your friends. Let's try drawing a treasure map first!

You will need:
- toothpick
- lemon
- small knife
- paper
- side plate, small container
- heat source, such as a light bulb or iron

What to do:

1 Ask an adult to cut a lemon in half for you. Squeeze the lemon juice into a small bowl.

2 The lemon juice is your "ink!" Dip the round end of a toothpick into the bowl.

3 Draw a secret map on some paper. Use lots of lemon juice for each part you draw.

4 Allow the paper to dry until you can't see the drawing any more!

What's going on?

The acid in the lemon juice breaks down the cellulose of the paper into sugars. The heat supplied tends to caramelize the sugars, making them brown and revealing the secret drawing.

5 Now move the paper back and forth under a heat source. As the ink gets warm, your secret map is revealed.

What else can you do?

Repeat this activity with vinegar or milk to find out which makes the best invisible ink.

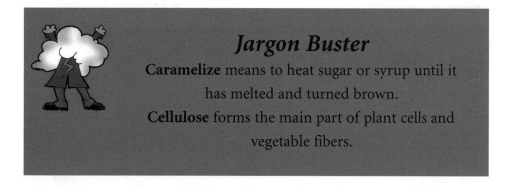

Jargon Buster

Caramelize means to heat sugar or syrup until it has melted and turned brown.

Cellulose forms the main part of plant cells and vegetable fibers.

Dense and denser

20 minutes

You will need:
- glass jar, 3 drinking glasses
- various liquids and solids: syrup, cooking oil, water, grape, plastic wine cork
- blue and red food coloring
- plastic dropper, coin

If we took similar sized cubes of wood and lead, the one made of lead would be much heavier. This is because lead is more dense than wood. It has more material packed into the same space.

The plan
We are going to compare the densities of different substances, then look at how temperature might affect density.

Experiment 1

cooking oil

water

syrup

1 Gently pour the cooking oil, syrup, and water into a glass, one at a time.

2 Let the liquids settle. They should form distinct layers.

3 We are going to put the grape, the coin, and the cork into the jar. Where do you think they will settle?

cork floats in oil

grape in water on top of syrup

coin sinks to base of syrup

What's going on?

The various substances float or sink according to their densities.

Experiment 2

1 Take a small glass of cold water and add some drops of blue food coloring. Put it in the refrigerator for an hour or so.

2 Take a small glass of hot water (from the faucet) and add some red food coloring.

3 Half fill a tall glass with the blue water from the refrigerator.

4 Use the dropper to transfer small amounts of the red water into the blue water. The idea is not to mix the two colors. Keep the end of the plastic dropper near the surface.

What's going on?

If you've managed to do this experiment carefully enough, there should be two distinct layers. What do you think the position of the layers tells us about their density?

Warm water is less dense than cold water, therefore the red colored water stays above the blue water in the glass.

Super goo

Here's how you can make an amazing gooey material that is like a cross between a liquid and solid.

You will need:

- 1 cup of cornstarch
- half a cup of water
- bowl, mixing spoon
- food coloring (just for fun)

The plan

We are going to find out how difficult it is to tell a solid from a liquid!

What to do:

1 Mix together the cornstarch, the coloring and the water. It should become quite thick, but still feel like a liquid.

2 Try stirring the mixture quickly and then very slowly. What happens?

Jargon Buster
Cornstarch can stand up to freezing or prolonged cooking!

3 Try to squeeze the mixture between your fingers. What happens?

4 Take some mixture in your hand and try to roll it into a ball.

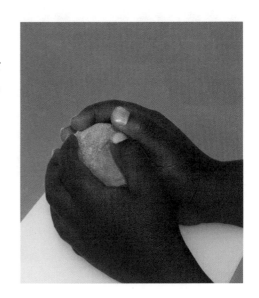

5 Put the ball down on a hard surface and hit it with your hand. (Be very careful with your hand!)

What's going on?

Cornstarch and water form a *colloid* rather than a solution. This means that the particles of cornstarch stay as a solid but are spread throughout the liquid. A colloid has unusual properties. You can stir it or let it run through your fingers like a liquid. When you try and move through it quickly (stirring fast) it resists. When you hit it, it shatters!

What else can you do?

Ketchup has colloid properties. What does this tell you about the best way to get it out of the bottle?

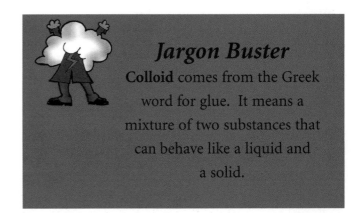

Jargon Buster
Colloid comes from the Greek word for glue. It means a mixture of two substances that can behave like a liquid and a solid.

Does air weigh anything?

30 minutes

You will need:
- 2 balloons
- string
- scissors
- thin piece of wood, about 2 feet long
- balloons, marker pen

The plan
To find out if air weighs anything.

What to do:

1 Make marks about ¾ inch from each end of the piece of wood.

2 Suspend the wood by a piece of string, so that it hangs horizontally. This is our weighing *balance*.

Jargon Buster
Air contains nitrogen, oxygen, argon, carbon dioxide, and water vapor.

3 Cut two pieces of string the same length—about 6 inches. Make a loop at the end of each piece, just big enough to slip over the wood.

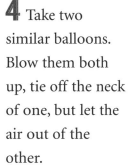

4 Take two similar balloons. Blow them both up, tie off the neck of one, but let the air out of the other.

5 Tie each balloon to one of the strings.

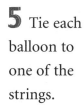

6 Slip the strings onto the stick, exactly on the ¾ inch marks.

What's going on?

The only difference between the two balloons is that one is "empty" and the other is full of air. But the air in the balloon is slightly compressed, so it is denser than the air around it, making the scale tip down.

What else can you do?

Try this puzzle! You'll need a kitchen scale and a glass of water. Place the glass of water on the scale: note the weight. Now, if you put your finger into the water without touching the glass, will the weight on the scale be more or less? Answer: see below.

Answer: More, because you add the volume of water displaced by your fingers to the weight.

Experiments with forces

Forces are involved in everything we do. When we make something move, we are in control of some forces and have to respond to others, often without knowing what they are! A force can be gravity, magnetism, or anything that exerts a push or a pull.

People have always known that objects fall downward. But the first person to understand that falling is caused by the force of gravity was Sir Isaac Newton. We'll look at gravity on page 30.

Since ancient times, scientists have used the idea of forces to try to explain the workings of everything from simple machinery to the courses of the planets. Over 4,000 years ago, the builders of Stonehenge in England seem to have placed the stones according to very careful *observations* of the stars and their movements.

At the CERN laboratory in Switzerland, scientists study the forces that hold together the universe.

Archimedes, a Greek scientist and mathematician from Syracuse, was set the task by King Hero II of finding out whether a new crown was made of solid gold, or if it contained silver. Knowing the *density* of gold, he needed to find the *volume* of the crown. He found the answer when he stepped into his bath—and displaced his own volume of water. If he submerged the crown and measured the displaced water, he could work out the crown's volume.

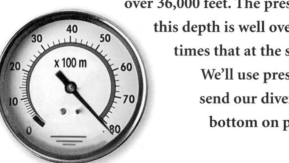

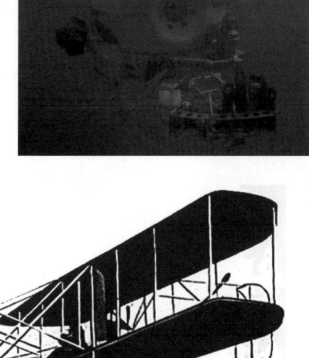

In the ocean between Japan and Papua New Guinea, the Mariana Trench is the deepest water yet surveyed, at over 36,000 feet. The pressure at this depth is well over 1,000 times that at the surface. We'll use pressure to send our diver to the bottom on page 35.

We'll use pressure to send our diver to the bottom on page 35.

Orville and Wilbur Wright's first controlled, powered, and *sustained* heavier-than-air human flight in 1903 traveled just 120 feet. Balancing the forces of power, drag, *lift*, and gravity remains the main thing that aircraft designers have to do. Test our design on page 42 and see if you can improve on it!

Test our design on page 42 and see if you can improve on it!

Down to Earth

20 minutes

All objects attract each other with gravity and the larger the object the larger the force. The Earth is huge and so has a strong gravitational pull.

The plan

We are going to see how gravity pulls objects towards the Earth, then look at a way to beat it!

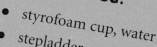

You will need:

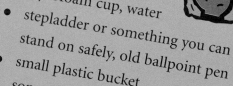

- styrofoam cup, water
- stepladder or something you can stand on safely, old ballpoint pen
- small plastic bucket
- somewhere outside to do the experiments

Experiment 1

1 Make a small hole with a ballpoint in the side of the cup near the base.

2 Fill the cup with water. See how the water runs out.

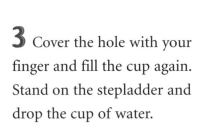

3 Cover the hole with your finger and fill the cup again. Stand on the stepladder and drop the cup of water.

What's going on?

Gravity makes the cup and the water *accelerate* down at the same rate. They fall together and the water stays in the cup till they hit the ground.

Experiment 2

1 Half fill your bucket with water.

2 Outside, swing the bucket forward and back. Increase the swing and make sure you don't spill any water.

What's going on?

When you swing the bucket, you apply a centrifugal force to the water in addition to gravity. The faster you swing, the greater the centrifugal force. When it's great enough, the water will stay in the bucket, regardless of gravity.

Jargon Buster
Centrifugal means moving away from the center.

3 When you get near the top of the swing, try going right over the top in a complete circle!

Balancing acts

25 minutes

When gravity pulls on an object, it appears to be acting on a single point which is called the center of gravity.

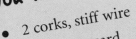

You will need:

- 2 corks, stiff wire
- plasticine, card
- universal glue
- toothpicks
- scissors
- marker pen
- fishing line
- plastic drinking straw
- chair, table

The plan
We are going to make objects with the center of gravity in unexpected places.

Experiment 1

1 Draw an outline of a head and body to fit the width of your cork.

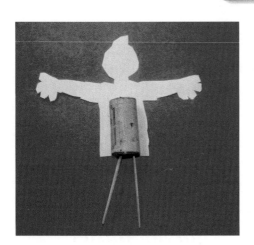

push through

bend and push back

2 Cut out the figure and glue it to the cork. Push the toothpicks into the cork for legs.

3 Ask an adult to cut a piece of wire 8 inches long. Bend it into a curve, add the plasticine weight, and fix it to the cork.

4 Adjust the amount of plasticine to get your figure to balance.

What's going on?

The plasticine makes the center of gravity lower than the surface of the table.

Experiment 2

Cut little slits here ...

... and here, so the arms can hold the pole.

1 Make up a new cork with wire and a plasticine weight as in Experiment 1.

2 Draw and cut out another little figure to fit on the cork. See how the feet are drawn.

3 Stick a piece of straw (about ¾ inch long) to the base of the cork and stick your figure on the front.

4 Thread the fishing line through the straw, then tie it between two fixed points to make a sloping tightrope. We used our cupboard door handles. Finish your tightrope walker with a balancing pole made from a straw.

What's going on?

This time gravity can pull the figure down, so it slides down the line. The straw pole is just for effect. It remains upright because its center of gravity is below the line.

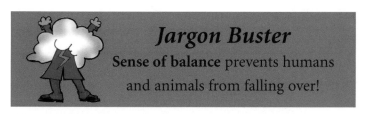

Jargon Buster
Sense of balance prevents humans and animals from falling over!

Under pressure

Pressure is a force that pushes against something. Pressure on a material forces its *molecules* closer together and it becomes denser. As material becomes more dense, it becomes heavier.

You will need:

- plastic bottle and stopper
- plasticine
- eyedropper
- water container for testing
- water

The plan

We are going to show what happens when gases and liquids are put under pressure. It's a famous experiment, called The Cartesian Diver, and we think it's fun!

What to do:

open end

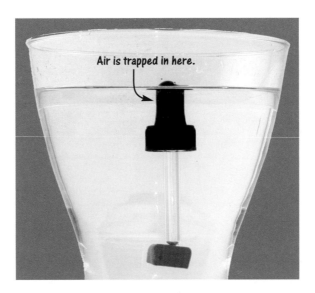

Air is trapped in here.

Seal the air inside the dropper with a blob of plasticine, which will also act as a weight.

Test the buoyancy of your diver in water. It should only just float. Add or remove plasticine till you get it exactly right.

Jargon Buster
Cartesian relates to the French scientist and thinker René Descartes. The experiment is named in his honor.

We've used the same amount of plasticine in two colors and made a head and legs.

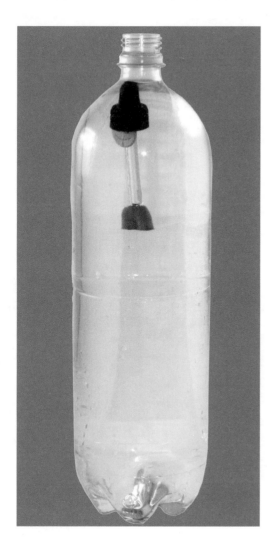

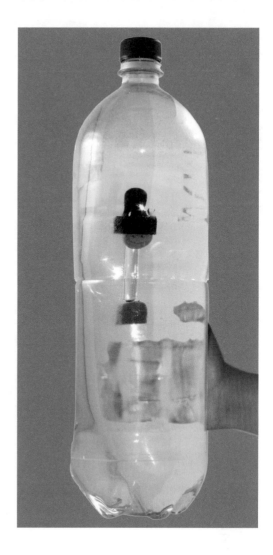

4 Fill the bottle with water. Put the diver in the bottle. Check that the diver is floating properly.

5 Screw the lid on tightly and squeeze the bottle. Your diver should move down in the bottle.

What's going on?

When the bottle is compressed, or squeezed, everything inside is put under increased pressure. Water is more dense than air and is harder to compress, so the air compresses much more than the water. At the start, the diver only just displaced his own weight of water. When the air is compressed it takes up less space and the diver displaces less than his own weight of water. When the pressure is released, he floats back up!

What else can you do?

Try making divers out of other things, such as pen tops, toys, or balloons. Remember, you must have some air in your diver that can't escape.

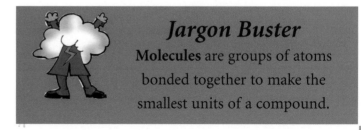

Jargon Buster
Molecules are groups of atoms bonded together to make the smallest units of a compound.

Jet propulsion

Hero's engine

We think of the jet engine as being a modern invention, but the first one was invented by *Hero of Alexandria* in the first century AD.

You will need:

- balloon (sausage-shaped)
- plastic drinking straw
- fishing line or fine string
- bulldog clip, tape
- empty fruit juice carton
- water, funnel
- old ballpoint pen
- somewhere outdoors

The plan

We're going to show how a jet engine works.

Experiment 1

1 Thread the fishing line or string through the straw.

2 Fill the balloon with air, then put the bulldog clip on the neck to keep the air in.

3 Fix the straw to the balloon with tape. Tie each end of the line to something fixed, at least 20 feet apart.

What's going on?

The air inside the balloon is under pressure caused by the balloon trying to go back to its original shape. When the clip is released, air escapes through the neck, and the balloon is pushed in the opposite direction.

4 Release the clip!

What else can you do?

Power toy cars or boats with balloons!

Experiment 2

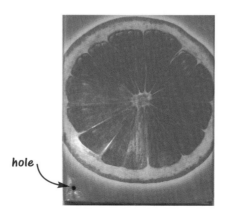

hole

1 Open the top flaps of the fruit juice carton and make small holes in them. Attach a loop of string between the flaps and another to the exact middle of the first string.

2 Make a hole in the front of the carton with the ballpoint pen, at the bottom on the left. Make a similar hole on the other side.

3 From here it's best to work outside! Cover the holes with your finger and thumb and fill the carton with water. You might need an assistant for this.

4 Hold the carton up by the string and uncover the holes.

What's going on?

The force of the escaping water on opposite sides drives the carton round in a circle, with the string acting as a pivot. We're using gravity and water to make jet *propulsion*!

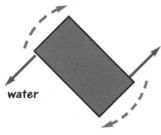

direction of rotation

water

Sink or swim?

35 minutes

If we drop a piece of metal into water, it sinks. So how is it that a ship made of material that's heavier than water, can float?

You will need:
- plasticine, paper clips
- water
- egg
- glass, jug
- salt
- tablespoon

The plan
We are going to find out how a ship floats.

Experiment 1

1 Knead a piece of plasticine into the size and shape of a golf ball.

2 Fill the jug with water, then drop the plasticine ball into it. It sinks!

3 Take the ball out of the water, and dry it. Then form it into a hollow shape.

4 Carefully lower the plasticine shape into the water again.

5 Your boat will even carry cargo!

What's going on?

Plasticine is much more dense than water so, in Step 1, it sinks. If you've managed to enclose enough space in your shape, it will float on the water. Archimedes discovered that an object will float when it displaces more than its own weight of water (see pages 28–29).

Jargon Buster
Displace means to take the place of.

Experiment 2

1 Half fill the jug with water and add about six tablespoons of salt. Stir it well to dissolve the salt.

2 Top up with plain water. Pour the water over a spoon so as not to mix it with the salt water.

3 Carefully lower the egg into the glass using the spoon. Try not to disturb the water!

4 The egg floats halfway down the jug!

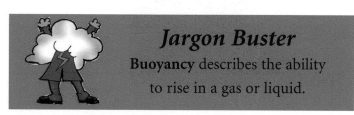

Jargon Buster

Buoyancy describes the ability to rise in a gas or liquid.

What's going on?

The egg is denser than plain water but less dense than salt water. The egg has buoyancy in the salt water, but not in the plain water, so it floats where the two kinds of water meet.

Cotton reel racer

You will need:

- long pencil
- rubber band
- empty cotton reel
- piece of candle
- paper clip, craft knife

We often need to store energy so that it is available exactly when we need it. Petrol and electrical batteries are examples of stored energy. Our bodies take in other forms of stored energy when we eat.

The plan

We are going to make a toy that uses stored energy to make it move. We call it a tank.

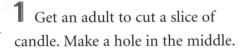

What to do:

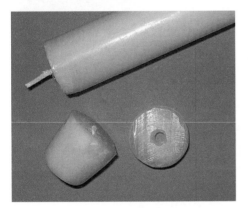

1 Get an adult to cut a slice of candle. Make a hole in the middle.

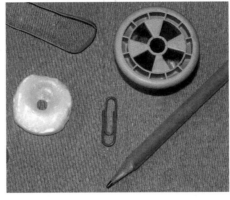

2 Push the rubber band through the cotton reel and attach the paper clip.

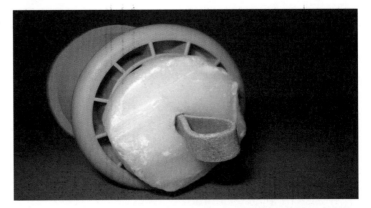

3 Thread the rubber band through the candle.

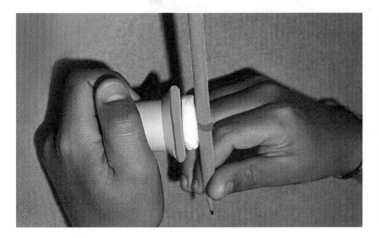

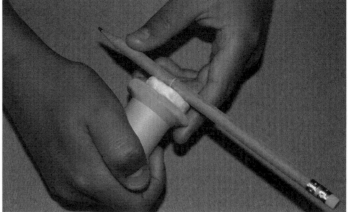

4 Put the pencil through the rubber band and wind it up as tightly as you can without breaking the band.

5 When the rubber band feels tight, put the whole thing on a level surface and release.

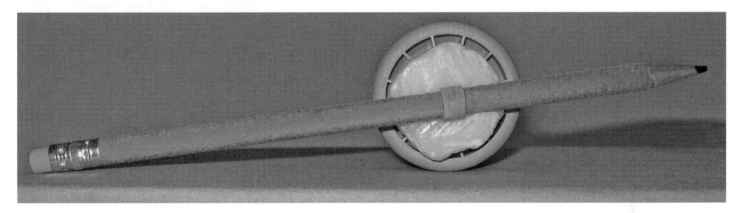

6 How far will it go?

What's going on?

We call the energy used to twist the rubber band in Step 4 *potential energy*. When we release the racer, the rubber tries to return to its normal length and, as it straightens, some of its potential energy is converted to movement (*kinetic energy*).

What else can you do?

Your racer will tackle rough ground better if it has notches round its edge. Get an adult to help with a craft knife.

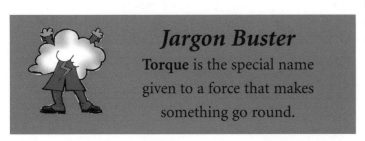

Jargon Buster
Torque is the special name given to a force that makes something go round.

Air force

How do planes stay in the sky? What invisible forces are at work to help them fly?

You will need:

- expanded polystyrene sheet (from a model shop), plasticine— about the size of a nickel, pin, thread
- black marker pen, scissors, glue stick
- colored paper, pencil, tracing paper
- an adult with craft knife, paints, brush

The plan

We are going to demonstrate how well a simple toy glider can fly through the air.

What to do:

1 Copy these three shapes onto a sheet of expanded polystyrene.

2 Carefully cut round the shapes with scissors. Ask an adult to cut out the two slots with a craft knife.

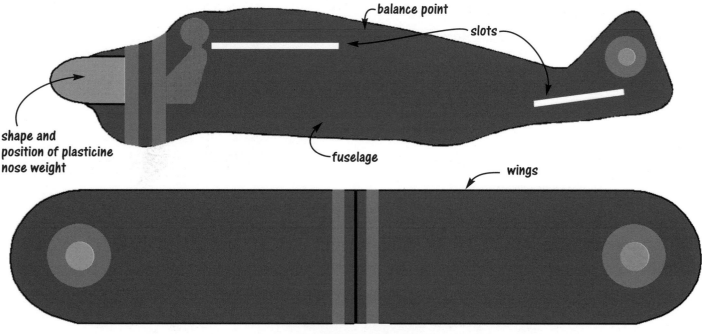

balance point

slots

shape and position of plasticine nose weight

fuselage

wings

tailplane

3 Paint the flat shapes first. Apply markings after paint is dry using colored paper shapes and a glue stick.

Add fine details such as body panels and canopy with a black marker pen.
Hang the plane from the balance point with a pin and some thread.

4 Check all paint and glue is dry. Push wings and tail into the slots. Add the plasticine to make a nose weight.

5 Adjust the position of the nose weight until the plane hangs correctly from the balance point. Launch the plane with the nose slightly down. Good flying!

What else can you do?

Help your friends to make planes and have a competition for the longest (timed in seconds), highest, and furthest flights!

What's going on?

The plane needs the forward motion of the launch to thrust it through the air. The wings passing through air convert this force to lift, opposing the force of gravity. The tailplane and tail fin stabilize the plane, keeping it at the right angle to stay up. If the plane loses forward movement through the air, it loses lift and drops.

Balloon fun

You will need:

- balloons, very large balloon
- permanent marker pen, string
- an assistant, wool sweater
- kitchen weighing scales

We've used balloons a lot in our experiments but there are still things they can show us. Here are two more forces at work.

The plan

We look at the difference between mass and weight, then see the force produced by a static charge.

Experiment 1

Here's a big, empty balloon. It weighs just ¾ ounce.

Scales are not accurate for weighing very tiny amounts.

What's going on?

The balloon doesn't seem to weigh any more after we've blown it up than it did before. But it feels heavier than the empty balloon would when it hits us because it carries the mass of the air inside it as well as the rubber of the balloon, all propelled by your assistant.

2 Now we've blown it up, and it seems to weigh about the same.

3 Your assistant takes the balloon and—while you're not looking— whacks you over the head with it!

Jargon Buster

Weight is how a mass is affected by gravity.

Experiment 2

1 Blow up two balloons and tie their necks. Attach strings.

2 With the strings at the top, draw a face on each balloon. Use a permanent marker so it doesn't smudge.

3 Find somewhere to hang them up—a doorway is ideal for this. Let them hang about 2 inches apart and see where they settle.

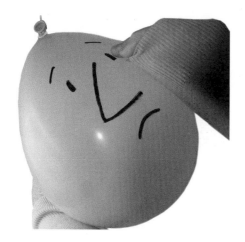

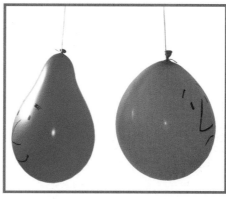

4 Rub the faces of the balloons with the wool sweater.

5 Let them hang free again and see how they behave.

What's going on?

In Step 3, the balloons settle with the faces pointing in any direction. In Step 5, the faces turn away from each other.

Rubbing a balloon with wool fabric produces an electrostatic charge on it. A similar charge on both balloons means that they will repel each other. The force should be strongest where the rubbing occurred, and so the faces turn away from each other.

Jargon Buster

Electrostatic charge is caused when an electrical charge is apparently trapped in an insulating material, such as the rubber of the balloon.

Experiments with light and sound

The main source of energy we have on the Earth comes to us as heat and light, across the near-vacuum of space from our nearest star, the Sun. Light is essential to life on Earth, and not just for us to see our way. Green plants must have light energy to change minerals into the chemicals they need to grow.

Many tools that use light, such as lenses and mirrors, interfere with its path and seem to bend it and make it change direction. They all work because light is very precise and predictable. Without interference, the way it travels is about the straightest line there is.

We'll look at mirrors on pages 48 and 49.

Ancient fortune-tellers used mirrors to make strange images appear in smoke. You can make your own *illusion* on page 50.

More than 300 years ago, Sir Isaac Newton, a scientist and mathematician, showed that sunlight could be divided into separate colors, always the same ones. Try a simple way of seeing the visible spectrum on page 48. You can try different ways of mixing colors back together on pages 49 and 54.

Unlike light, sound needs a material to pass through. Our voices are carried through air, but sound can travel through other materials too. Look at pages 56 and 57 for ideas.

A foghorn is a warning for ships at sea when it's too foggy to see properly. Experience proves that lower notes work best, but it's still hard to know what direction a sound is coming from. See what happens when you try to hear round corners on page 62.

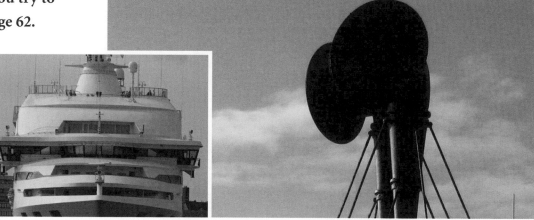
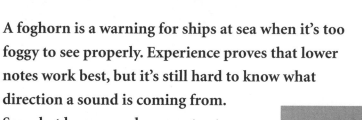

Rainbows

40 minutes

You will need:

- large bowl, scissors
- water, clear plastic bottles
- plastic mirror, marker pen
- colored plastic or candy wrapper
- white card, string, colored papers, paints, old ballpoint pen

Have you ever wondered how a rainbow is formed? Daylight, or "white light," is actually made up of lots of different colors mixed together, called the visible spectrum. A rainbow is formed when white light passes through droplets of water in the air.

The plan

We are going to make a spectrum from white light and a spinner you can make from card and string!

Experiment 1

1 On a sunny day, take the bowl outside and fill it with water.

2 Put the mirror into the water and reflect sunlight up and onto the white card. Move the mirror around until you find the best angle.

3 The reflected light should look something like this.

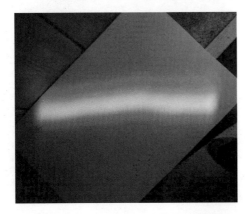

Jargon Buster

Remember the colors of the spectrum by learning this saying:
Richard of York gave battle in vain—
red, orange, yellow, green, blue, indigo, violet.

What's going on?

Light passes from air to water, strikes the mirror, and passes back out to the air again. Light is refracted each time it goes between different materials. The colors that make up white light are each refracted at slightly different angles. The result is the visible spectrum—red, orange, yellow, green, blue, indigo, and violet.

What else can you do?

Use a sheet of colored plastic or candy wrapper and hold it between the Sun and the water. What happens to the refracted light?

Experiment 2

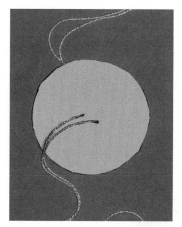

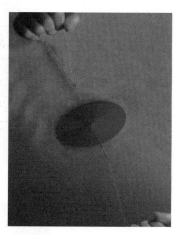

1 Draw round a lid on a piece of stiff white card. Now cut out the disc with scissors.

2 Make two holes in the middle with a ballpoint pen. Thread the string through and tie the ends.

3 Paint green and red on one side, or stick on two pieces of colored paper.

4 Now spin the spinner! When the strings twist, pull gently. What colors can you see?

What's going on?

Your eye cannot react fast enough to each color in turn so you see a blend of the two colors.

What else can you do?

Try painting the disc with different colors. What new colors can you see?

Pepper's ghost

45 minutes

Here's an experiment that's part science and part magic trick, and all about not necessarily believing what we see. It gets its name from "Professor" John Pepper, the 19th-century scientist who perfected this effect.

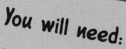
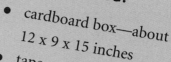

You will need:

- cardboard box—about 12 x 9 x 15 inches
- tape
- sheets of stiff black paper
- clear plastic—same size as one face of box
- tea light with holder, matches
- card tube—about 3 inches in diameter and 6 inches tall, sheet of card
- glass of water, glue stick, paints, brushes

The plan
We are going to reveal the secret of Pepper's ghost.

What to do:
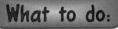

1 Measure 1 inch in from the edges of one side of the box and cut a window.

2 Using the glue and tape, line the inside of the box with black paper, except for the window. Fix the plastic over the window with tape.

3 Ask an adult to help you cut a piece out of the card tube, about a quarter of its *circumference*, from top to base. Line the inside of the rest of the tube with black paper.

4 Light the tea light and place it in front of the box. Fill the glass with water. Find the position of the virtual image of the tea light and put the glass inside the box.

5 Position the tube so that the candle is totally screened from the front.

6 Now view the effect from the front. The candle should seem to be still burning underwater!

What's going on?

Normally we can see straight through clear plastic and in daylight it appears as if all the light goes through. In fact, a small amount is reflected, but in daylight it's too faint to see.

In our experiment, we've constructed a special arrangement where all you see is lit by the candle. We've placed the glass exactly so that the candle's virtual image (its reflection in the plastic) is in the same place.

What else can you do?

Use your box to make more "magical" effects. Create a 19th-century Victorian theater by copying this one onto thin card. Fix the decorated card to the front of the box. Put cut-out photographs of friends in place of the candle, and photographs from magazines of unusual places in the box. You'll need two small torches to make it work. Good luck! Gather an audience to watch your show!

Light trap

25 minutes

Light can only travel in straight lines—but it's possible to bounce it inside of a material like water. You can use this technique to make it travel along a stream of water!

You will need:

- glass or glass container
- water, a little milk
- plastic bottle with a screw top
- kitchen foil, kitchen sink
- flashlight, water, tape
- small screwdriver
- a friend to help you
- kitchen you can make dark

The plan

We are going to show how fiber optics work.

Ask friends to help.

Experiment 1

1 Fill a glass container with water. Add a few drops of milk.

2 Put some kitchen foil round the end of your flashlight and make a slit in it.

3 Darken the room. With the slit horizontal, shine the flashlight up through the side of the glass, adjusting the angle until light reflects down from the surface of the water.

Experiment 2

1 Cover the bottle with foil, using tape to hold it in place. Leave the base of the bottle uncovered.

2 Make a hole in the side of the bottle near the top.

3 Cover the hole with your thumb and fill the bottle with water.

4 Replace the screw top. Keep your thumb over the hole. Turn the bottle upside down. Hold the lit flashlight against the base.

5 Get your friend to turn off the lights. Remove your thumb from the hole. The water escaping should pick up light from the flashlight.

What's going on?

In Experiment 1, when the angle between the surface of the water and the light beam is great enough, light is reflected back.

In Experiment 2, because of the large angle at which the light hits the boundary between the stream of water and the air, it is reflected back into the water. When it hits the other side of the stream, the same thing happens. This is called total internal reflection. The light only escapes when the water stream hits the sink and scatters.

Color mix-up

20 minutes

We know that when we mix two different colors of paint together we get a third one. The colors we get when we mix colored light are quite different.

The plan

We are going to compare two ways of mixing color.

You will need:

- white card, torch
- colored paints and brushes
- clear plastic sheet in different colors—buy from a craft shop or try candy wrappers
- notebook and pencil
- darkened room

Experiment 1

1 Mix up three patches of thick color—blue, red, and green.

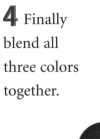

2 While the paint is wet, use a clean dry brush to blend the edges of the patches together. First blend blue into red.

3 Then clean your brush and blend red into green.

4 Finally blend all three colors together.

What's going on?

The blends between the three colors are muddy and less bright than the colors that make them.
Paint is made to absorb all the other colors of light and only reflects its own.

Experiment 2

1 This time we're going to use colored plastic to filter the light from a torch.

2 Work in a darkened room. Shine your torch onto white card. Try the colored filters one at a time, then try combining two or three. Write down your results.

3 Try red and blue. You should see magenta.

4 Blue and green makes cyan (turquoise).

5 Green and red make yellow.

What's going on?

The results are quite different from those produced by using paint. Mixing our red and blue paint produced a dull brownish purple. When we add red and blue light, we get a bright magenta.

What else can you do?

Find combinations of filters that block the light.

Jargon Buster
A filter allows only part of a spectrum through it.

Secret sounds

45 minutes

Sound travels to our ears through the air by making the molecules in the air vibrate, but it can also pass through solid materials in the same way.

You will need:

- a friend to help you
- string, metal objects (for example cutlery or a coat hanger)
- clean, empty yogurt pots
- hammer and nail

The plan

We are going to show that sound can pass through solid materials.

Find a friend.

Experiment 1

1 Tie the ends of two lengths of string to objects and hold the other ends against your ears.

2 Swing the object so that it bangs against something (could be a wall) or get your friend to hit the spoon with something solid. Now try using both objects.

What's going on?

When the object is hit, it vibrates, making a sound which we can hear normally. As we are suspending the objects on taut string, the vibration will travel up the string, making it vibrate. Because we have our fingers pressed into our ears, we can't hear normally through the air, but we can hear the transmitted vibration coming up the string.

Experiment 2

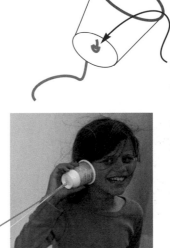

Knot the string inside each yogurt pot. Pull the string tight between the pots.

1 Get your string and two clean yogurt pots ready to make a great telephone.

2 Ask an adult to make a hole in the base of each pot with a hammer and nail, then fix a long piece of string between the pots.

3 Give the other pot to a friend. Stand some distance apart, keep the string tight, and listen or speak!

4 How long can you make the string and still hear the person at the other end?

Experiment 3

Next time you are in a wood, look for a felled tree and get your friend to press an ear against one end. Go to the other end and gently gently tap or scratch against the trunk. How small can you make that noise before the other person can't hear you?

Jargon Buster

Transmit means to pass something from one place to another.

Seeing sound

25 minutes

Of course we can't actually see sound, but we can see its effect!

The plan

We are going to show that sound travels in waves.

You will need:

- large bowl, plastic wrap
- 2 large empty plastic bottles
- plastic sheet, cut from a carrier bag
- tape, feathers, tissue paper, rice
- container used for savory snacks
- hammer and nail, scissors, balloon

Experiment 1

1 Stretch some plastic wrap over the top of the bowl. Sprinkle some dry rice grains over the surface of the plastic wrap.

What's going on?

The sound of the plastic bottles banging together *transmits* through the air in waves and causes the plastic wrap to vibrate, bouncing the rice up and down.

Jargon Buster

The **decibel (dB)** is the unit used to measure sound level.

2 Bang two plastic bottles together!

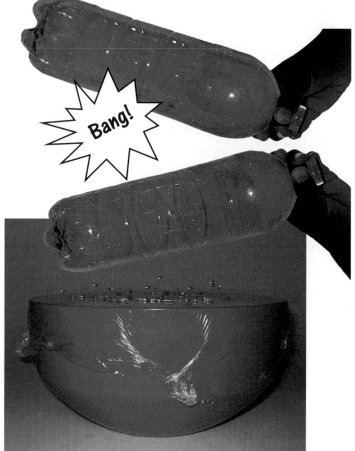

Bang!

Experiment 2

1 Ask an adult to make a hole in the closed end of the container. We used a nail and hammer.

2 Take the piece of carrier bag plastic and stretch it over the open end of the tube. Hold the piece of plastic firmly in place with sticky tape.

3 Point the end with the hole toward the feathers or little bits of tissue paper. Tap the plastic at the other end sharply.

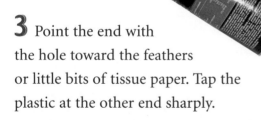

What's going on?

When you hit the plastic, the sound waves pass down the tube and out through the hole, moving the feathers. This is the shock wave that causes damage in an explosion.

What else can you do?

Hold an inflated balloon against your ear and ask someone to speak very close to the other side. You can feel the vibrations.

In tune?

Sound is produced in lots of ways. Here's a method of producing different sounds using the same equipment.

You will need:

- several similar glass bottles
- water, food coloring (optional)
- paper and pencil
- stick or ruler

The plan

We are going to see how sounds of differing pitch are produced.

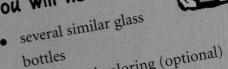

1 Fill the bottles with water to different levels. Put the bottles in a line and in order—most water to least water. We've colored ours, but it's not necessary for the experiment.

2 Test them for pitch by striking each bottle (gently) with a stick. Strike each bottle in the same place.

3 Use the same set of bottles. Now blow across the top of each bottle in turn. Try and get a clear note.

What's going on?

Sound is made by creating vibrations in a material. These vibrations are carried through the air to our ears as waves.

In Step 2, the sound is made by a sharp blow of the stick making the combination of water and glass vibrate. The more water there is in the bottle, the lower the pitch, and the less water, the higher the pitch.

In Step 3, the sound is made by vibrating a volume of air. The greater the volume of air, the lower the pitch, and the smaller the volume of air, the higher—exactly the opposite result to Step 2.

What else can you do?

You could make two sets of bottles to play tunes with a friend—one set for hitting, one for blowing!

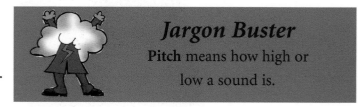

Jargon Buster
Pitch means how high or low a sound is.

Bouncing sound

35 minutes

Sound can be reflected in much the same way as light.
It's what happens when you hear an *echo*.

The plan

We are going to find out whether sound follows
the same rules as light when it is reflected.

You will need:

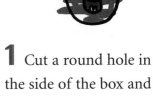

- a friend to help you
- 2 cardboard tubes (from kitchen foil or similar), notebook, pencil
- stiff card, shoe box, scissors
- sticky tape, ticking clock

1 Cut a round hole in
the side of the box and
fit a tube to it.

2 Put the box and tube on
a table. Place the sound
source (the clock) inside
the box.

3 Put the other tube on the table with one end near the open end of the first tube.

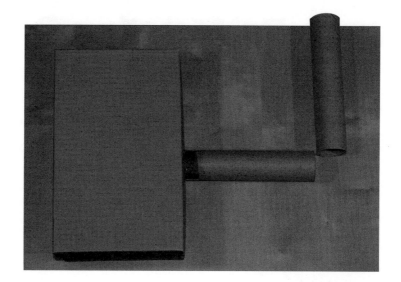

4 Put your ear to the end of the tube and get your assistant to hold a piece of cardboard where the ends of the tubes meet. Note the position of the card when you can hear the clock best.

What's going on?

The sound is funneled down the first tube and reflected by the card into the second tube, but only if the angle between the card and both tubes is the same—just like light.

What else can you do?

Try using different materials instead of the card to see if some things reflect better than others.

Seeing round corners

You will need:

- empty carton—clean, dry fruit juice carton or similar size box, universal glue
- 2 plastic mirrors—each about 3 x 2 inches
- ruler, scissors, parcel tape, marker pen

The *periscope* is a device that uses mirrors to let us see round things. It's a good way to see over the heads of crowds!

25 minutes

The plan

We're going to make a simple periscope.

What to do:

1 Remove any plastic spout and seal the box with tape. Measure the depth of the box (**D**) and mark the same distance up the side.

2 Measure the diagonal (**X**). Using the ruler, draw the outline of a square flap on the bottom of the front of the box (black line). Take care to use the same measurement (**X**) for the height and width of the flap.

small plastic mirrors

3 Carefully cut three sides of the flap and fold inward. Use sticky tape to fix the flap at a 45° slant.

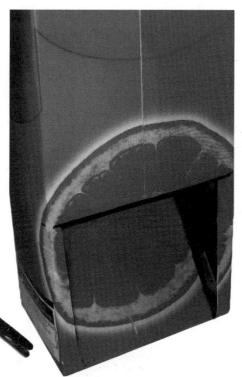

4 Cut a flap at the top of the box on the other side, the same size (**X** by **X**) as before. Fix this flap, again at a 45° slant, with tape.

5 Stick one mirror to each flap with some universal glue.

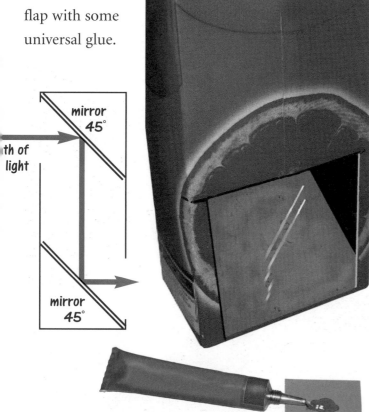

6 Now test your periscope!

See next page for how to decorate your periscope!

What's going on?

Light travels in straight lines. The first mirror changes the direction of the light by reflecting it, then the second mirror changes it back, parallel to its original path.

What else can you do:

Why not decorate your periscope? Use colored paper to cover your box, and fix it in place with glue sticks. Don't cover either of the viewing windows!

Take your periscope to sports events—you will be able to see over other spectators' heads! When it is decorated you can keep your periscope as a toy.

Experiments with heat

Heat is a form of energy. On Earth, most of our heat energy comes from the Sun, even though it is 92 million miles away.

thermometer

The *temperature* scales most commonly used in science are Fahrenheit (°F) and Celsius (°C). Water boils at 212 °F / 100 °C, and *freezes* at 32 °F / 0 °C. The lowest possible temperature where no heat energy at all remains is – 459.67 °F / –273.15 °C, known as **absolute zero.** It is a theoretical point that can't quite be reached, but scientists can get very close to it!
We make a thermometer on page 79.

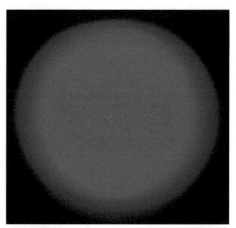

The temperature on the surface of the Sun is about 9932 °F / 5500°C.

Pompeii worm

All forms of life need heat to survive, but not always the same amount. In the frozen soils of Alaska and Siberia, there are tiny life forms called microbes which survive and grow in temperatures well below freezing (– 4 °F / –20 °C). Meanwhile, under the sea, around deep ocean vents, the Pompeii worm lives and thrives in water at 176 °F / 80 °C. How does the walrus cope with freezing sea temperatures? See our experiment on page 74.

Heat energy can move from one place to another in different ways. Look at our experiments on *conduction*, *convection*, and *radiation*.

hot air balloon

radiant heater

heat conductors inside a computer

Hot topic: conduction

25 minutes

Conduction is the way heat is carried through solid materials—for example, from a kitchen hob through the saucepan to the food.

The plan

We are going to find out which materials are best at conducting heat.

You will need:

- hot water (tea kettle)
- mug
- assortment of long thin objects made of different materials, such as:
  table forks and spoons
  wire coat hanger
  plastic drinking straw
  knitting needles
- clock that shows seconds

What to do:

1 Get an adult to help you heat some water.

Jargon Buster
Heat can pass easily through a good **conductor**.

2 Put some hot water in the mug. Be careful!

3 Stand the first object in the water. Hold the other end. See how long it takes to become too hot to hold.

4 Fill the mug with hot water again and try other things. This time we're testing a metal coat hanger.

5 Now it's a plastic drinking straw.

6 This is a wooden spoon.

What's going on?

Energy in the form of heat passes from one molecule to the next along the object. Metals conduct heat well and so are called good conductors. Nonmetals, like plastics and wood, are not good conductors and are called *insulators*.

What else can you do?

Try comparing results for objects made of the same material, but of different thicknesses.

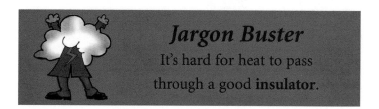

Jargon Buster
It's hard for heat to pass through a good **insulator**.

Moving story: convection

45 minutes

The way that heat is carried through liquids and gases is called convection. An example of this is a radiator heating up a whole room.

The plan

We are going to show a convection current in air by using *smoke*.

You will need:

- shoe box with a lid
- two paper towel tubes
- tea light in a holder
- one popsicle stick
- sticky tape • scissors
- thin card • matches
- thread

What to do:

1 Draw two circles on the lid of the shoe box, one toward each end. Draw round the end of the paper towel tube.

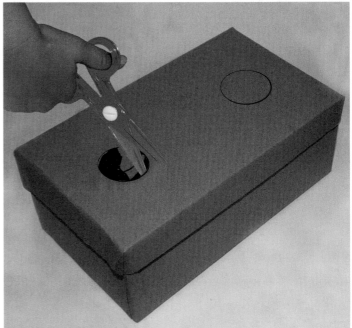

2 Cut the holes out and stick the tubes in place with sticky tape.

3 Light the tea light and put it in the shoebox so that it is under one of the tubes when the lid goes on.

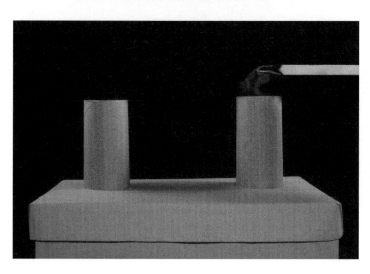

4 Light the end of the popsicle stick with a match (ask an adult to help). Then blow the flame out.

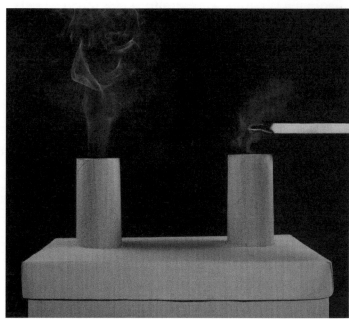

5 Hold the glowing stick over the tube that doesn't have the tea light under it.

6 Smoke goes down the tube and eventually comes out of the other.

What's going on?

The candle flame heats the air, which rises up through the tube. Cooler air is heavier and is drawn down the other tube. Air travels through the box, drawing the smoke with it.

What else can you do?

Copy this spiral shape onto thin card and cut it out with scissors. Attach a thread to the middle and hang it up. Put a tea light under it—not closer than 8 inches—and watch the rising air make it spin!

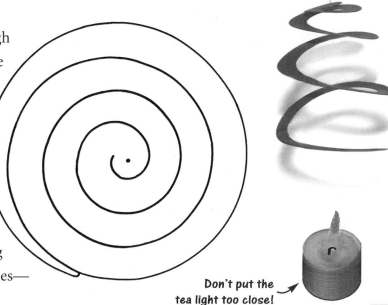

Don't put the tea light too close!

Warming glow: radiation

30 minutes

Radiation is the only form of heat that can travel through a vacuum. An example is the way heat gets to us from the Sun, through space. The heat we feel from a desk lamp is also radiation.

You will need:

- thermometer
- desk lamp
- different, contrasting materials: for example, things that are light or dark, shiny or matt, cut into pieces of a similar size and shape
- sticky tape

The plan

We are going to show how different substances absorb heat radiation.

Experiment 1

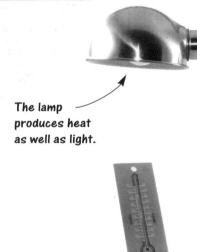

The lamp produces heat as well as light.

Find a place to work where the temperature is fairly even. Keep away from direct sunlight and room heaters.

2 We are using a desk lamp as a source of radiant heat. Put your thermometer under the lamp.

3 Note the temperature rise after 10 minutes.

Jargon Buster

A **vacuum** is space that contains absolutely nothing.

What's going on?

Heat is getting to the thermometer by radiation. It is a way in which heat travels as waves of energy.

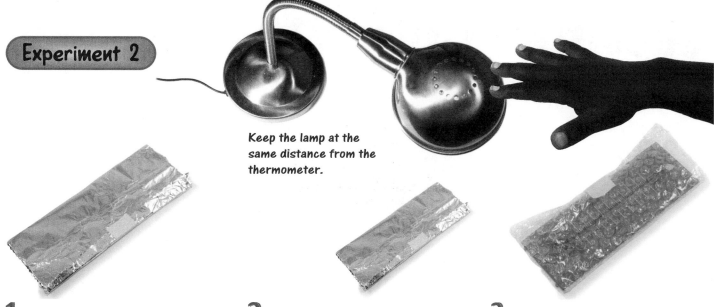

Experiment 2

Keep the lamp at the same distance from the thermometer.

1 Start with the thermometer at room temperature again. Wrap it in a fold of test material. This is kitchen foil, which is very thin aluminum sheet. Hold it in place with sticky tape.

2 Put the wrapped thermometer under the lamp. Note the temperature after 10 minutes, then at 10-minute intervals.

3 Let the thermometer cool back to room temperature, then repeat with other materials. You can try combinations, too!

4 Make a graph to show your results. It should show that shiny material insulates against radiant heat better than matt. Lighter material insulates better than darker material.

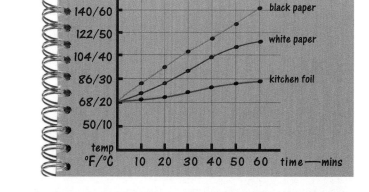

What's going on?

Dark, matt surfaces absorb these waves and soak up the heat. Light, shiny surfaces reflect the waves and stay cooler.

What else can you do?

Can radiation pass through solids? Try putting a sheet of card, glass, or plastic between the radiator and the thermometer.

Jargon Buster

Radiant heat is heat given off by something hot. **Radiation** is a general word used for energy that travels in waves. **Radiator** describes something that gives off energy. The radiators in our homes give off heat by a mixture of radiation and convection.

73

Blubber glove

25 minutes

How does a walrus keep from freezing? Why are walruses covered in wobbling blubber? Let's make a *blubber* mitten and find out!

The plan
You're going to find out for yourself how well fat works as an insulator.

You will need:
- supply of thin plastic sandwich bags
- soft *margarine* at room temperature
- plastic dishpan
- ice cubes, spoons
- hair *stretchies*, string, or wool to put around your wrists
- watch or clock that shows seconds
- assistant

1 Scoop margarine into a plastic bag.

2 Put one hand into another plastic bag. Use your left hand if you're right-handed, or your right hand if you're left-handed.

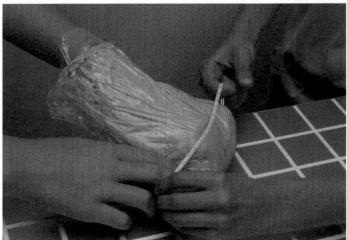

3 Spread a thick layer of margarine over the bag. Now put this hand into the bag that already has margarine in and squish the margarine around so that it covers your hand. This is your "blubber mitten."

4 Ask your friend to fasten the mitten with big rubber bands so that they don't slip off—but not too tight. Put two empty plastic bags on the other hand and fasten these, too.

5 Fill the dishpan with cold water and ice cubes.

6 Put both hands into the ice water. Don't let water into the bags. Use the watch to time how long you can keep each hand in the water before it gets uncomfortable.

What's going on?

The margarine insulates, keeping the warmth of your hand in rather than letting it pass to the water. Animals that live in very cold areas have thick layers of fat called blubber under their skin to keep their bodies warm.

What else can you do?

You could try wearing a woollen or padded glove on the hand that doesn't have the blubber mitten. Use a plastic bag to keep it dry. Can you keep the hand in for longer than with just a bag? Which is a better insulator, blubber or the fabric glove?

The Water cycle

Nature has its own water recycling system we call the water *cycle*.

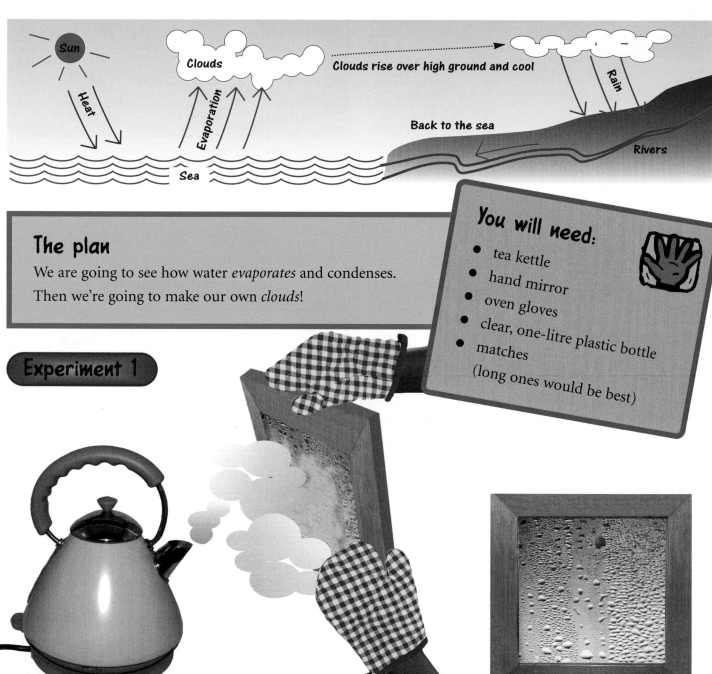

Sun

Clouds

Clouds rise over high ground and cool

Heat

Evaporation

Rain

Back to the sea

Rivers

Sea

The plan

We are going to see how water *evaporates* and condenses.
Then we're going to make our own *clouds*!

You will need:

- tea kettle
- hand mirror
- oven gloves
- clear, one-litre plastic bottle
- matches
  (long ones would be best)

Experiment 1

1 Fill a tea kettle half full of water and start heating it.

2 When it begins to boil, turn the kettle off, and use the oven gloves to hold the mirror in the steam.

3 You should soon see water droplets form on the surface of the mirror.

What's going on?

The element in the kettle heats the water until it starts to change from a liquid (water) to a vapor (steam). The steam is less dense than water and takes up more space, so it pushes its way out of the kettle. Steam touching the surface of the mirror is quickly cooled, and changes back to water.

Experiment 2

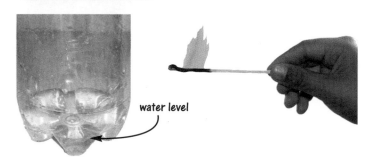

water level

1 Put enough warm water in a bottle to cover the bottom. Light a match and let it burn for a few seconds before blowing it out.

2 Immediately, hold the match in the neck of the bottle to catch as much smoke as you can.

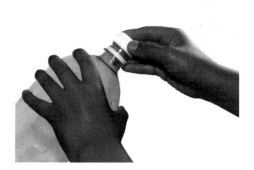

cloud shapes

3 Quickly put the cap on the bottle so as not to lose any smoke.

4 Squeeze the bottle eight or nine times (more may be necessary).

5 When you release the bottle, you should see little clouds forming inside.

What's going on?

Some of the warm water evaporates inside the bottle. Releasing the pressure in the bottle slightly cools the air inside so some of the water vapor changes back to liquid droplets. The smoke particles help them to form. Clouds are just collections of water droplets.

Jargon Buster
A **droplet** is a very small drop of liquid. A **particle** is a very small amount of something solid.

Bigger and hotter: expansion

25 minutes

When things get bigger, they are said to expand. Things expand when they are heated and when they are cooled, they contract, or get smaller.

The plan
We are going to make our own thermometer.

You will need:
- plastic bottle
- plastic drinking straw
- plasticine, thermometer
- warm water
- food coloring
- saucepan, stove

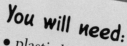

plasticine seal

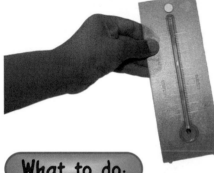

This thermometer is made of glass and plastic. It has a special red liquid inside it.

What to do:

1 Fill the bottle to the brim with cool water mixed with a few drops of food coloring.

2 Seal the straw into the neck with plasticine, with most of the straw outside the bottle.

The water has risen from here to here!

3 Put the bottle in a saucepan of warm water. Heat moves from the water in the pan to the water in the bottle. Water rises up the straw a little.

4 Gently heat the pan. Get an adult to help you with this. As the water in the pan gets hotter, the water rises higher in the straw.

What's going on?

When the water is heated, it expands. The only way it can go is up the straw. The hotter it becomes, the more it expands, so the further up the straw it goes.

What else can you do?

Compare your thermometer with a commercial one. Make sure it's the kind that can go into very hot water. Use the readings from the commercial thermometer to label your new thermometer.

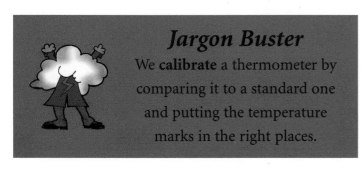

Jargon Buster
We **calibrate** a thermometer by comparing it to a standard one and putting the temperature marks in the right places.

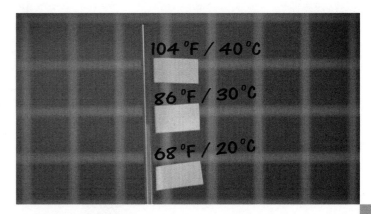

104 °F / 40 °C

86 °F / 30 °C

68 °F / 20 °C

Mighty ice

24 hours

In the last section, we said that most things contract when they cool. However, when water freezes it expands!

The plan

We are going to see why it is important not to let your water pipes freeze in the winter.

You will need:

- 2 large plastic bottles
- 1 small plastic bottle
- water
- freezer

Experiment 1

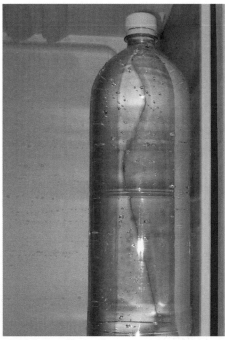

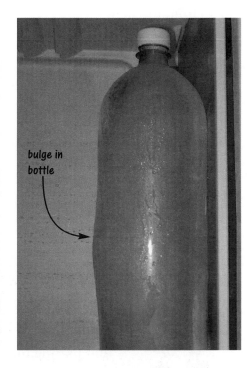

bulge in bottle

1 Fill the bottle to the top with cold water and fasten the cap.

2 Place it in the freezer and leave it there overnight.

3 By the next morning, the bottle will be swollen. It may even have split open!

What's going on?

When water freezes, it forms ice crystals which occupy more space than water molecules. For the same volume, ice is less dense than water. Water is very unusual in this. Most liquids become more dense as they cool. Water is at its most dense at 39.2 °*Fahrenheit* / 4 °*Celsius*.

An iceberg is lighter than the water it floats in, so that one-tenth of it is above the water.

Experiment 2

How can we check that one-tenth of floating ice is above the water? Iceberg shapes are very hard to measure!

4-6   8-12

base of ice block

1 Use two plastic bottles, one a little smaller than the other. They need to be fairly straight-sided. Cut the top off the larger one. The smaller one should just fit inside it.

2 Fill the smaller one with water, but only as far as where it starts to narrow. Place it in the freezer overnight, standing upright.

3 In the morning, get an adult to help you cut the bottle off the ice with scissors. Put some water in the larger bottle and float the ice block in it. You can now measure how much is standing out of the water.

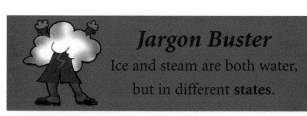

Jargon Buster
Ice and steam are both water, but in different **states**.

Antifreeze

24 hours

Have you ever wondered why we put salt on the roads when it's icy or snowing?

The plan

We are going to see what effect adding salt to water has on the way it freezes.

Experiment 1

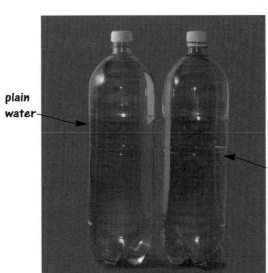

plain water

salt solution

1 Make some salt solution. Add salt to water until no more will dissolve.

2 Fill a bottle to the top with salt water and another with the same amount of plain cold water. Put them both in the freezer overnight.

3 In the morning, only the plain water has frozen.

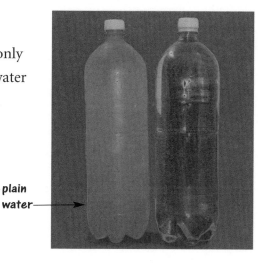

plain water→

What's going on?

Impurities in water, in this case salt, lower the freezing point so the water remains liquid.

Experiment 2

Here's a little trick you can try using ice.

1 Put a cube of ice in a glass of plain water.

2 Pour a little salt onto the cube.

3 Hang the end of a piece of thread so that it lies on the salty patch and leave it for a few minutes.

4 After a while, you'll be able to pick up the cube with the thread! The salt makes the ice melt, then it freezes again around the thread

Jargon Buster
A **solution** is a mixture of two or more substances. Table salt dissolved in water is a solution.

Disappearing act

30 minutes

When we put certain things like salt or sugar into water, they seem to disappear. In fact, they are still there, but have dissolved.

The plan

We are going to see how temperature affects dissolving.

You will need:

- salt
- small saucepan
- two spoons
- thermometer
- water, stove

What to do:

Add salt, one spoonful at a time, to a small saucepan of cold water.

Use another spoon to stir the water. Count how many spoonfuls can be added before no more will dissolve.

3 Repeat with the water at different temperatures, using the same quantity of water and same size spoon each time. You'll need an adult to help when you're using hot water. Be careful when touching the stirring spoon—if it is metal, it may get quite hot.

4 Leave the hottest pan of water to cool.

What's going on?

The hotter the water, the more salt it can hold in solution. When you let the water cool, the salt cannot stay in solution, and it falls out as salt crystals on the bottom of the pan.

What else can you do?

See if the same thing happens with other solids. You could try different kinds of sugar, sand, or even chalk dust!

sand

white sugar

crushed chalk

brown sugar

Jargon Buster

When one substance **dissolves** in another, the result is a **solution**.

Experiments with plants and other living things

Living things include plants, animals, *fungi* (like mushrooms), and algae (like seaweed). Other living things are tiny organisms such as *bacteria* and protozoa which can be seen only with a microscope. Living things can be found in every type of habitat on Earth—on land and in lakes, rivers, and seas.

Arctic lupin

Plant seeds can live a long time. The record for the world's oldest germinated seed is an arctic lupin (lupinus arcticus). Found in a lemming burrow in frozen Arctic tundra, the seed actually grew after 10,000 years!

A lemming in its burrow

Rafflesia flower

Scientists think that there are over a million species of fungi in the world, but only about 10 percent have been properly described.

Fungus

The rainforests of Borneo are home to the world's biggest flower, called the rafflesia. It's a parasitic plant with no stem or leaves, but with roots buried in the tissue of its host vine. It needs flies to spread its pollen to other flowers, so it attracts them by producing the smell of rotting meat!

Man belongs to a group of animals called mammals. The smallest mammal is the Kitti's hog-nosed bat, from Thailand, around 1¼ inches long and weighing only about 0.07 ounces. The largest mammal is the blue whale, weighing up to 200 tons and around 108 feet long!

Blue whale

Kitti's hog-nosed bat   Algae

Algae have *chlorophyll*, like plants, and manufacture their own food from *nutrients* and sunlight. Scientists used to think they were a kind of plant, but now they're seen as a separate kind of life.

Here's another amazing plant seed fact. A seed from an Asian water lotus (Nelumbo nucifera) was grown after 1,200 years.

Asian water lotus

Bacteria have a very simple form of life, but they can really thrive in the environment to which they are adapted.

Bacteria grown in the laboratory

Like plants, bacteria, and algae, you and your friends are
LIVING THINGS!

Jargon Buster
A **mammal** is an animal that has a backbone, hair, or fur and gives birth to live young which it feeds with milk.

What do seeds need to grow?

Many plants spread themselves by scattering seeds. A seed contains a new plant and enough food for it to start growing.

20 minutes

You will need:

- paper towel
- thick cardboard
- 4 clean, shallow food trays
- quick-germinating seeds, such as cress
- water

The plan

We are going to find out what else a seed needs to germinate—water, light, warmth? You'll need to collect some food trays for this project.

What to do:

1 Put three or four thicknesses of paper towel in the bottom of each tray. Scatter the same number of seeds in each tray. Label them A, B, C, D. Wet the paper towels in trays A, B, and C.

A
has water, light, and warmth

B
has no warmth and no light

C
has no light

D
has no water

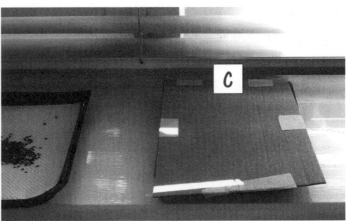

2 Put trays A and D near a window in a warm room.

3 Cover tray C with thick cardboard to keep the light out and put it with A and D.

4 Put tray B in the fridge, to give no warmth.

5 Check the trays daily. After five days the seeds should look quite different. (See "What's going on?")

What's going on?

Seeds won't germinate without water, but they don't need light. Without warmth, they grow more slowly or don't germinate at all.

What else can you do?

Keep the germinated seedlings in the same conditions and see if their needs are the same.

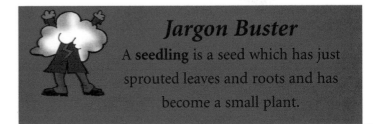

Jargon Buster
A **seedling** is a seed which has just sprouted leaves and roots and has become a small plant.

Which way is up?

Have you ever wondered why, when you plant seeds, the roots always go down into the soil and the leaves up into the air?

25 minutes

You will need:

- 4 glass jars, fava bean seeds
- some paper towels or blotting paper
- scissors, water

The plan

We're going to germinate some seeds in different positions to see which way the roots go.

Start with four bean seeds from the packet.

What to do:

1 Cut a piece of paper towel or blotting paper to fit round the sides of the jar—so that it fits snugly against the sides.

Jargon Buster
Germinate means begin to grow and put out shoots.

The black scar where the bean was attached to its pod.

2 Find the black scar on each seed. Put one seed in each jar, between the glass and the blotting paper.

Make each bean lie in a different direction. The first with the scar up; the second with it down; the third with it to the left; the fourth to the right.

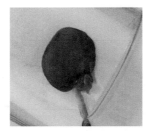

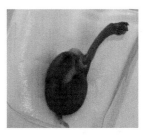

3 Put about 1 inch of water in each jar. It should soak into the paper to reach the seeds. Keep the water at this level.

What's going on?

The roots and the shoots always grow from the same point on the seed, but they react to gravity. Roots grow with gravity; shoots grow against gravity.

What else can you do?

After they have germinated, turn the seeds so that the roots are pointing upward and see what happens.

Thirsty flowers

45 minutes

Plants get their water from the soil, but where does it go from there?

You will need:

- freshly cut white flowers; carnations are ideal
- glass of water, plastic dropper
- food coloring, scissors
- magnifying glass

The plan

We are going to see where water goes in plants by using dye to follow its path.

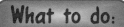
What to do:

1 Drop some food coloring into a glass of water.

2 Trim the flower stem before putting the flower into the water. Leave the flower for a while and see what happens.

3 You should get results something like this!

Giant redwood trees in America

What's going on?

Plant stems are made up of long hollow cells like a series of drinking straws. As water evaporates from the leaves, water is drawn up the plant from the soil. This occurs

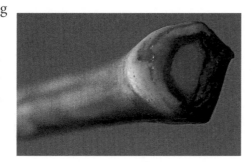

in all plants. Giant redwood trees grow to more than 350 feet and draw water up their trunks in this way.

Jargon Buster

Transpiration means evaporation from leaves drawing water into a plant.

What else can you do?

Try dyeing colored flowers and see what new colors you get, test a red flower and green dye.

Use a magnifying glass to examine flower stems to check out the details close up!

The perfect place for plants

Have you ever wondered if plants like some kinds of soil more than others? By testing with *seedlings*, we try to find out where they grow best.

45 minutes

You will need:

- 4 same-size seedlings
- 4 similar containers
- compost, sand, gravel, soil
- water, labels, pen, notebook

The plan

We are going to see how seedlings develop when planted in different types of growing material.

What to do:

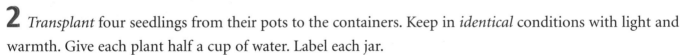

1 Put compost, sand, gravel, and garden soil into similar sized containers. We have used clean glass jars.

2 *Transplant* four seedlings from their pots to the containers. Keep in *identical* conditions with light and warmth. Give each plant half a cup of water. Label each jar.

compost

sand

gravel

soil

94

3 After a week you should be able to see clearly which plants are *thriving* or failing. Do you know why?

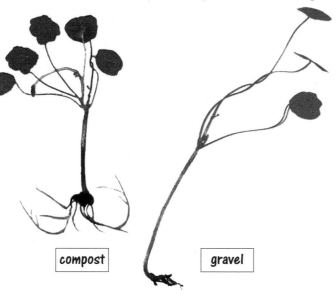

4 Remove the BEST plant from the jar to check the root structure. Notice that both the leaves and the roots are *developing* well. This plant **likes** the conditions you have provided.

5 Remove the WORST plant from the jar to check the root structure. The plant is weak. Notice that both the leaves and the roots are not developing well. This plant **does not like** the conditions you have provided.

What's going on?

Results should prove that plants prefer a mixed material to grow in, such as garden soil or compost. They will not grow as well in sand or gravel, which provide no nutrients.

What else can you do?

After you have finished observing the plants, find a good place for the healthy ones in a garden so that they have a chance to flourish.

House for a louse

45 minutes

You probably have a house that's dry, warm, and light—but would that suit other animals?

The plan
We are going to find out what sort of conditions woodlice like to live in!

You will need:
- 5 cardboard boxes (all about the same size and shape, such as tissue boxes)
- 4 cardboard tubes, 2 plastic carrier bags
- 2 pieces of cardboard, plastic wrap
- paper towels, sticky tape, marker pen
- at least 15 live woodlice (look under stones)
- scissors, water, notebook, map pin

What to do:

1 Place a cardboard tube on the long side of a tissue box. Draw round the tube with a marker pen.

2 Cut out the circle with scissors. Repeat the process on three more boxes. On the last box you will need to mark and cut out a hole in each side.

3 Cut out the top of all five boxes, leaving a ½ inch border around the edge. Mark the boxes A, B, C, D, and E.

4 Line the bases of all the boxes inside with plastic sheet cut from a carrier bag, then put in two layers of paper towel. Dampen the paper in boxes A and B.

5 Stretch plastic wrap over two of the boxes, A and C. Use thick card, cut to the right size, to cover two more boxes, B and D. Use tape to fix the covers.

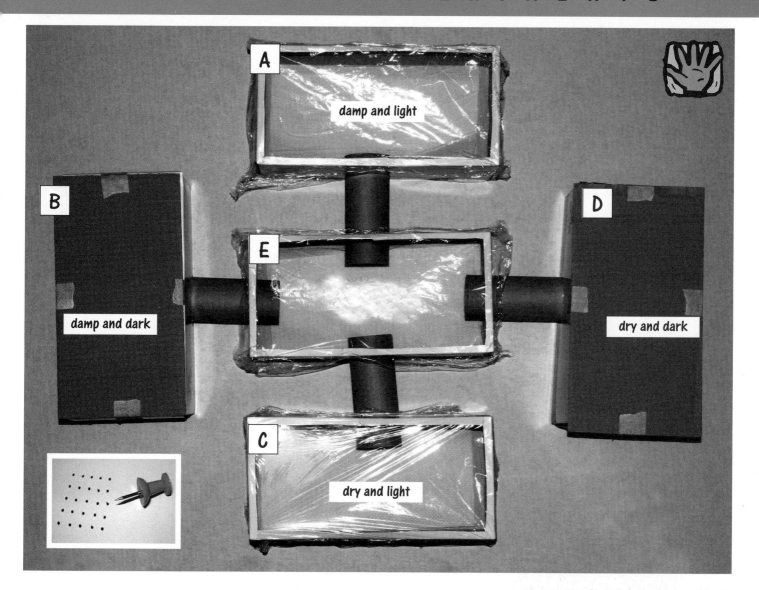

6 Push the tubes into each box and connect them up as shown in the photograph above. Fix the tubes with tape. Make pin holes in the sides of all boxes for air (see inset picture above).

7 Place the woodlice in box E and cover the box with plastic wrap. Over a period of four days, carefully check the numbers of woodlice in each outer box to see which one they prefer! Make notes of results.

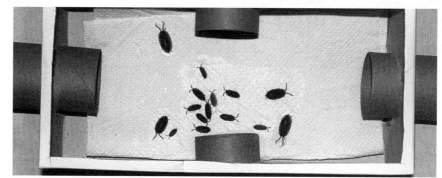

What's going on?

Like plants, animals are adapted to different living conditions—what suits one could kill another.

Very important!

Put the woodlice back where you found them once you have finished observing them!

A Wormery

60 minutes

We know that worms live under the ground. What do they do there? And why are they popular with gardeners?

You will need:

- 2 sheets of clear plastic about 12 inches square
- 3 pieces of wood 1 x 2 inches thick cut to the following lengths: 1 piece x 12 inches, 2 pieces x 11 inches
- strong waterproof tape
- universal glue, scissors
- sand, soil, leaves, grass, and earthworms

The plan

We are going to make a wormery.

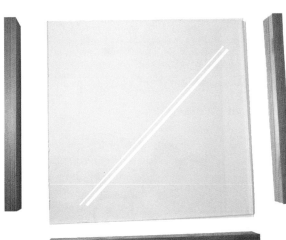

What to do:

1 Assemble the bits of the wormery as shown here.

2 Lay one sheet of plastic on a table, put the longest piece of wood at the base. Fix with universal glue. Add the two sides.

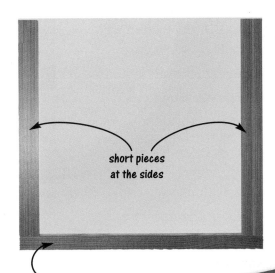

short pieces at the sides

long piece of wood at the base

Jargon Buster

Lumbricus terrestris is the scientific name for the earthworm.

3 Allow the glue to dry completely. Spread more glue on the surface of the wooden frame to fix the second piece of plastic. This completes the box. But you could tape all round the frame for extra strength.

4 Add soil and sand in 1 inch layers. Dampen the sand with water. Put the worms on the top layer with some leaves and bits of grass for food. Keep the soil damp and do not over-water.

5 Observe the wormery over several days and weeks. Make notes about the results.

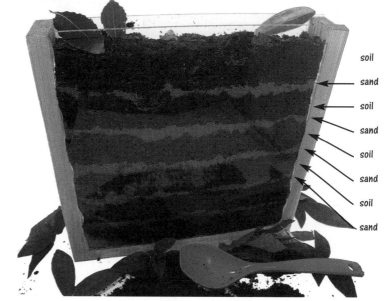

soil
sand
soil
sand
soil
sand
soil
sand

worms move the layers around

worms drag the leaves underground

What's going on?

The worms mix up the soil as they move about and feed. They also break up lumps of soil and dry leaves, which become food for plants. Their burrows allow air into the soil, which also helps break down plant material. All these activities improve the soil, so most gardeners like worms in their garden.

What else can you do?

Put tiny pieces of grated vegetables on the top layer to check if your worms like a varied diet!

Very important!

When your experiment is finished, return your worms to the place you found them.

Seeing things

20 minutes

So far we have experimented with some of the living things in the world around us. But we are alive, too, and we can also experiment on ourselves!

The plan

We are going to learn a bit about how our eyes work and how using two eyes is often better than one!

You will need:

- small table
- large sheet of paper for the target
- 3 different colored thick-tip marker pens, a tin lid
- scissors and thin card for the spinner
- pencil, glue stick
- string

Experiment 1

1 Draw your target on paper and put it flat on a table.

2

 Cover one eye.
To test your aim, hold a marker pen with the top removed, at arm's length. Try to drop it on the center of the target.

Cover the other eye.
Repeat the test and try to hit the target with the next marker.

Use both eyes.
Repeat the test with the last pen.

Experiment 2

1 Draw round a tin lid with a marker. Cut out two discs from your card to make a spinner.

2 Draw a simple bird cage on one disc and a black bird on the other one. Stick the discs together, back to back, with one drawing upside-down.

3 Make a hole on each side of the card and tie a string to each hole. Holding the strings, flip the circle of card so that the strings twist over and over.

4 Pull the strings tight so that the disc spins back and forth quickly. As you watch you will see the two drawings combine—now the bird is in the cage!

What's going on?

In Experiment 1—are some marks off target? Each eye sees things from a slightly different angle. The brain compares the two different images and works out how far away objects are. With only one eye it cannot do this.

In Experiment 2—an image of what we see remains on the retina of the eye for a fraction of a second after the object disappears. Because the movement of the card is so rapid, the image is still there when it has spun round, so we see both sides of the card at once.

Jargon Buster

Stereoscopic vision means seeing something with both eyes. Each sees the same area from a slightly different angle. The eyes' views have plenty in common, but each eye picks up visual information the other doesn't.

Find that sound!

The sense of hearing has qualities that we often take for granted. Here's an experiment that shows how our ears help us find our way around.

Get friends to help you!

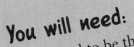

You will need:

- a friend to be the "subject"
- 12 feet of plastic hosepipe
- 2 plastic funnels
- blindfold
- notebook, pen or pencil
- some more friends

The plan

We're going to see how well we can tell the direction a noise is coming from, without relying on our eyes.

What to do:

1 Cut the hosepipe in half. Push a funnel into each hose.

2 Get a friend or classmate to stand in an open space. Put a blindfold around his or her eyes. They now become "Subject A" for your hearing experiment! Position the other people around them, without letting the subject know where they are.

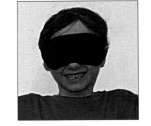

3 In turn, each person claps their hands together once. After each clap the subject must point in the direction of the noise. Do they guess right or not?

Clap!

Clap!

Clap!

Clap!

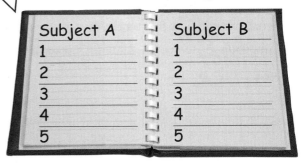

Subject A	Subject B
1	1
2	2
3	3
4	4
5	5

4 Write down the results in your notebook to compare with the answers in the next part.

5 Keep the subject blindfolded. He or she becomes "Subject B." Ask the subject to hold the ends of both the hosepipes to their ears. Get two people to hold a funnel each and point it in random directions.

6 Repeat Step 3, but this time the subject must turn to face the direction they think the noise is coming from. Record the answers in your notebook.

7 Compare your results for Step 3 and Step 6. What difference do the hosepipes and funnels make to the answers?

What's going on?

Just as we use both eyes to form a picture of the world around us, we use both ears to identify the direction from which a sound is coming.

What else can you do?

Test how easy it is to find the direction of a sound with only one ear. Put a hand over the other ear. Then get a friend to help you find the direction of the sound with the hose and funnel!

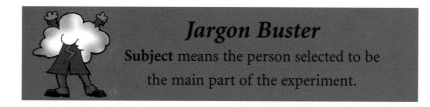

Jargon Buster

Subject means the person selected to be the main part of the experiment.

Mystery box

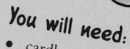

Touch is another important sense we rely on to keep us safe. It lets us experience sensations like hot and cold, rough and smooth, wet and dry, soft and hard.

The plan
To see if your friends can identify hidden objects by touch alone.

What to do:

1 Cut two holes in the sides of the cardboard box, big enough to get your fist through. Decorate the box with colored paper or marker pens.

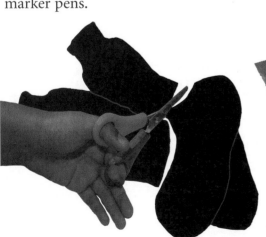

Use the tape inside the box to fix sock "sleeve."

2 Cut the straight bits off two old black socks (ask before you ruin dad's best footwear). Use strong tape to fix them on the inside of the box, so they make "sleeves" coming out of the box. Put your hands through the socks to feel the objects in the box without seeing them.

Experiment 1

1 Collect some objects, such as a spoon, a tennis ball, toys, fruit, a pencil, a cotton reel, a pine cone, sunglasses, a slipper, a brush, aluminum foil, keys, an oven glove, and an empty match box.

2 Put several things in the box at the same time, without anyone else seeing. You can either have two people playing using one hand each, or one person using both hands.

3 Ask how many items are in the box . To help them guess an object ask questions: "Is it heavy?" "Is it light?" Discuss the texture of objects: smooth, rough, bumpy, soft, hard, and so on. Record results to see who gets the most right.

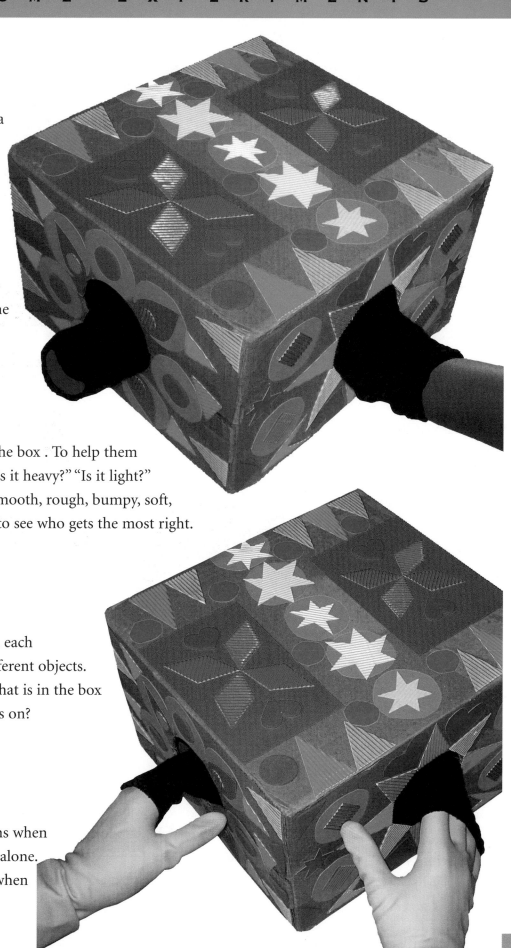

Experiment 2

Wearing a pair of rubber gloves, each person has another go using different objects. Again, everyone tries to guess what is in the box this time. Is it harder with gloves on?

What's going on?

You can now judge what happens when you rely on your sense of touch alone. It's harder to recognize objects when you can't see them.

Experiments with electricity and magnetism

From the earliest times, human beings have marveled at the sound and power of electricity in the forms of thunder and lightning.

Now electricity is essential for modern life. Look around your home. Count how many things you can find that work by electricity.

How many of these things need electricity to work?
How many of these things have magnets in them?

brains

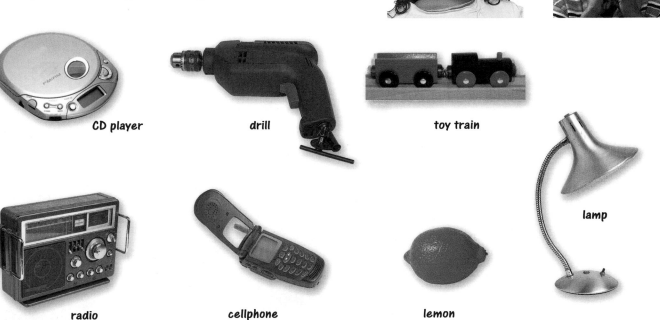

CD player

drill

toy train

lamp

radio

cellphone

lemon

Answers: They all need electricity to work except the lemon and the toy train. However, we'll be using the lemon to make electricity later on in the book.

Anything that has an electric motor or a loudspeaker has magnets. So there are magnets in everything except the lamp (or the lemon!). The toy train has magnetic couplings.

We make electricity from other forms of energy. We can burn fuel, such as coal or oil, or use natural forces such as wind or water.

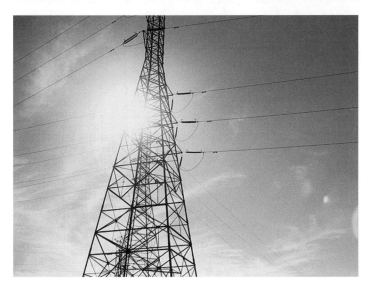

Electricity is carried to where it is needed by metal cables. The cables are held up on big towers called pylons. The thicker the cables, the more electricity they can carry.

In our home, we connect things to this supply of electricity through plugs and sockets, and the electricity flows through smaller wires.

In our experiments we're going to use batteries. Later on, we'll make our own electricity (see page 116).

Long ago, *magnetism* was thought to be a form of magic. Early navigators, such as the Vikings, used a special piece of magnetic rock, called a lodestone, as a *compass* to help them find their way in strange seas.

You will need a compass when you get to page 124.

a piece of lodestone

Making a circuit

Electricity is carried in a *circuit*. A circuit is a kind of loop through which electricity flows.

The plan
We are going to make our own circuit.

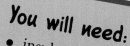

You will need:
- insulated wire
- MES bulb and bulb holder,
- sticky tape
- battery (AA)
- board
- scissors
- paper clips
- drawing pins

Circuit diagram

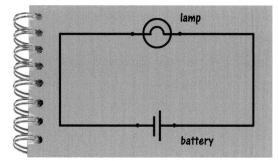

lamp

battery

Jargon Buster
A **lamp** is made up of a bulb and a bulb holder.

What to do:

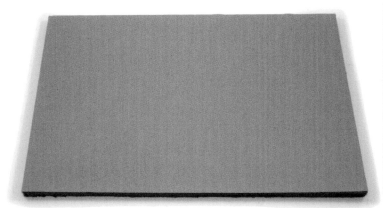

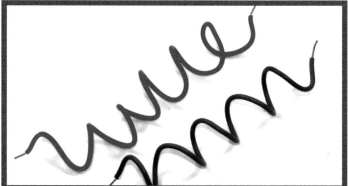

1 We need a piece of board to build our circuit on. This is a piece of softboard. You could use wood or plywood. Make it about 12 x 8 inches.

2 Prepare your wire by stripping the colored insulation from both ends. You can do this with a pair of scissors, but you'll need an adult to help.

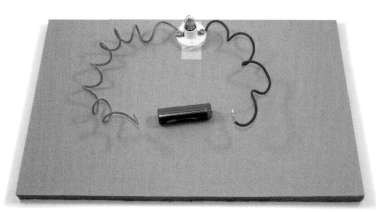

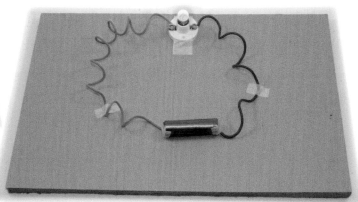

3 We've fixed the lamp to the board with some sticky tape to make things tidier.

4 Fix one end of each wire to the lamp and the other ends to the battery using sticky tape.

What's going on?

The lamp comes on because we've made a continuous circuit connecting the battery and lamp. If the lamp doesn't come on straight away, try turning around the battery.

What else can you do?

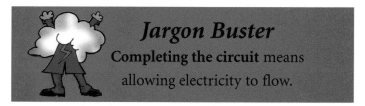

Use two paper clips (not plastic coated) and two drawing pins to make a battery holder like this.

The battery should be held firmly in place between the paper clips.

Jargon Buster
Completing the circuit means allowing electricity to flow.

Alternatively, you can use a battery holder to give a reliable fixing point for the wires.

Go with the flow

Which materials can electricity flow through? Those which allow electricity to pass through them are called conductors. Those that don't are called insulators.

35 minutes

The plan

We take the circuit we built on pages 108 and 109 and use it to find out whether materials are conductors or insulators.

You will need:
- the circuit from page 109
- ballpoint pen
- plastic comb
- nail
- flower
- string
- coin

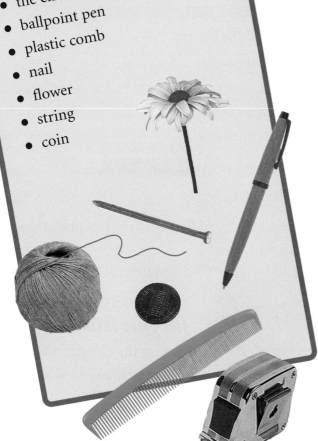

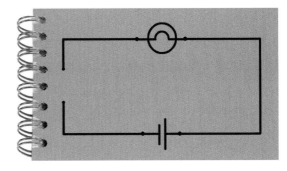

What to do:

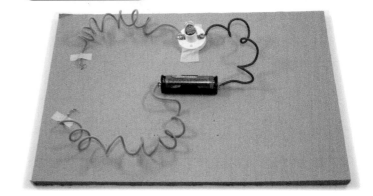

1 Add a new wire to the circuit we made on page 109. We've decided to use a battery holder this time.

2 We are going to use the ends of the wire to test different materials.

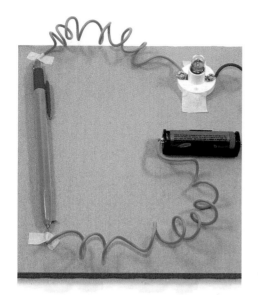

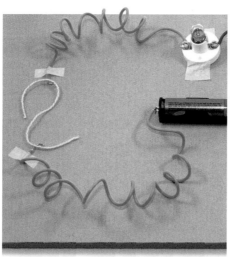

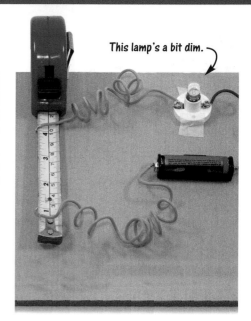

This lamp's a bit dim.

3 A plastic pen doesn't complete the circuit.

4 Neither does the string.

5 The paint on the tape measure is resisting the current.

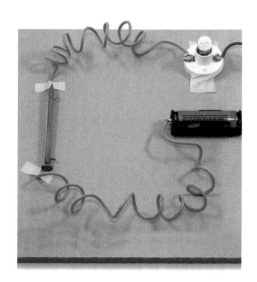

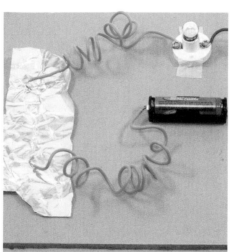

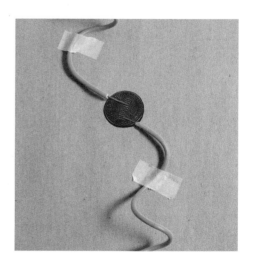

6 This nail completes the circuit.

7 So does aluminum foil.

8 Will this coin complete the circuit? What about the flower?

What's going on?

Most conductors are metal. We use insulators such as plastics to stop electricity going where we don't want it to go.

What else can you do?

Look at these tools. Why do you think they've got thick rubbery handles?

Switch on!

30 minutes

We've made a circuit that lights lamps but we probably don't want it to be on all the time.

The plan

Let's make a simple switch to turn the lamp on and off.

You will need:
- the circuit we made in the previous pages
- 2 drawing pins
- a paper clip

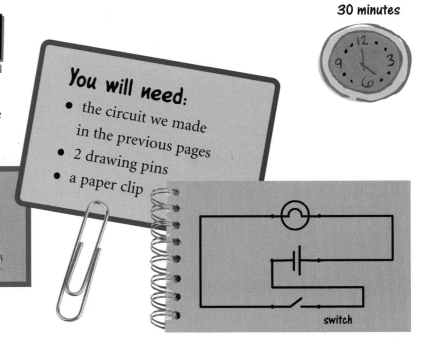

switch

What to do:

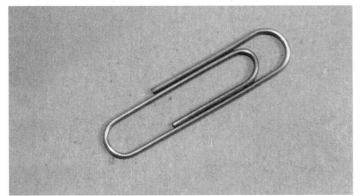

1 Your paper clip must be made of metal and not painted or coated with plastic.

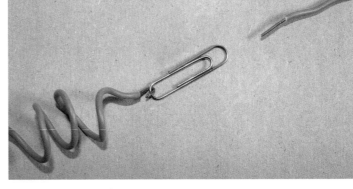

2 Test the paper clip as a conductor by the method we used in the last experiment.

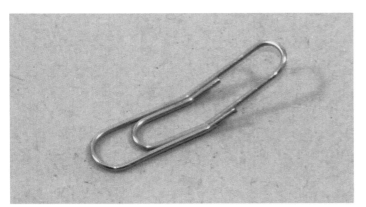

3 Bend the paper clip a little in the middle.

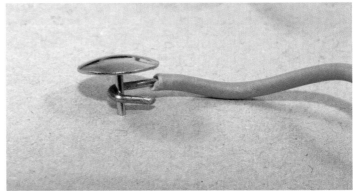

4 Bend the bare wire end of one of the wires round a drawing pin and press it into the softboard.

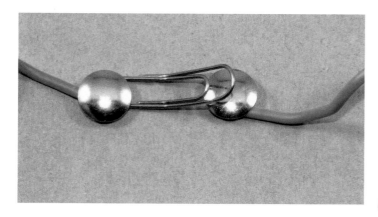

5 The other drawing pin holds the other wire and the paper clip in place.

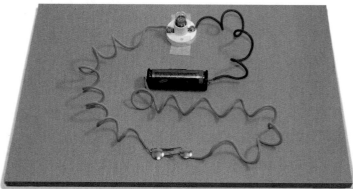

6 Here's the switch in the circuit.

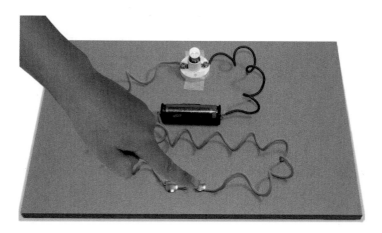

7 Press the switch to turn the lamp on!

What's going on?

Electricity flows when there's no break in the circuit.

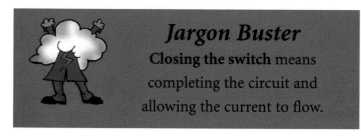

Jargon Buster
Closing the switch means completing the circuit and allowing the current to flow.

What else can you do?

We made a switch that has to be held down to keep the switch closed. You can use the same components to make a switch that stays closed.

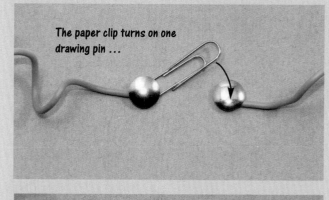

The paper clip turns on one drawing pin ...

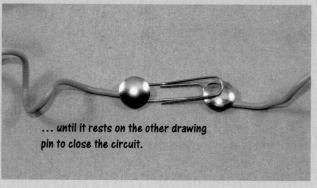

... until it rests on the other drawing pin to close the circuit.

Bright ideas

40 minutes

What happens when we want more light? Do we make more circuits like the one on the last page, or can we just add more lamps to the circuit? Let's find out!

The plan

We are going to connect more bulbs to the circuit.

You will need:

- the circuit from the last experiment
- 2 more bulbs and lamp holders
- 2 short lengths of wire with insulation stripped from the ends

Experiment 1

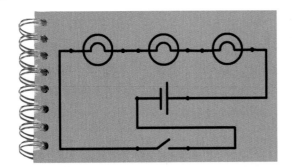

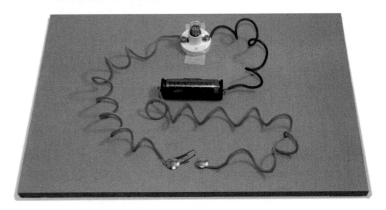

1 Take the circuit we made on pages 112–113. Make sure the switch is turned off.

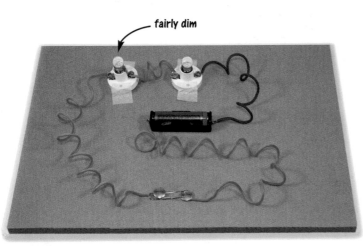

fairly dim

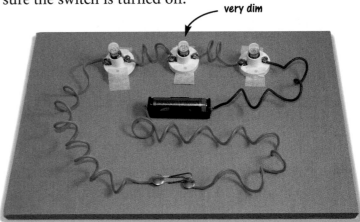

very dim

2 Connect another lamp in the circuit next to the first one. Switch on the current.

3 Switch off and connect another lamp to the circuit to make three. Switch on again.

What's going on?

We've connected the bulbs together in the circuit like a daisy chain. This is called a series circuit. Every bulb we add to the circuit increases the energy required for the electricity to flow.

Lamps in series

Experiment 2

There's another way to use electricity in a circuit, in parallel. Let's see what difference it makes to the result.

Lamps in parallel

quite bright

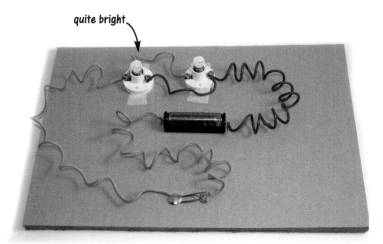

just as bright

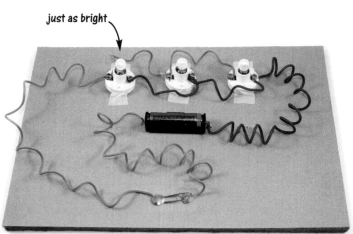

1 Start as in Step 1, page 114. Connect one more lamp in the way shown above, using two more wires. Switch on.

2 Switch off and connect a third lamp with two more wires, as in the diagram below. Switch on again.

What's going on?

This time we've connected the lamps in parallel. Each bulb in the circuit gets the right amount of electricity to make it work. The battery might not last for long running three bulbs, though.

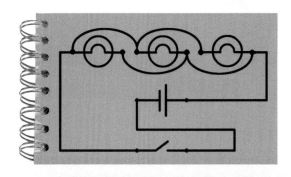

What else can you do?

We wanted more light—it seems we'll need more power! Let's look at batteries in the next section.

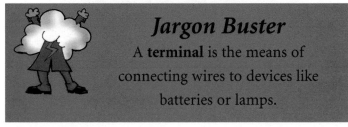

Jargon Buster
A **terminal** is the means of connecting wires to devices like batteries or lamps.

The lemon battery

When you've got tired of buying fresh batteries for your experiments, here's a way of making your own. The trouble is, you may have to buy some lemons instead!

You will need:
- three popsicle sticks
- aluminum kitchen foil
- 3 lemons
- 8 paper clips
- 3 pieces of copper tube about 4 inches long
- insulated wire
- an old calculator with an LCD
- small knife

The plan
We are going to produce electricity and power a device using fresh fruit!

What to do:

Get an adult to cut a square hole and a slot in each lemon with a small knife.

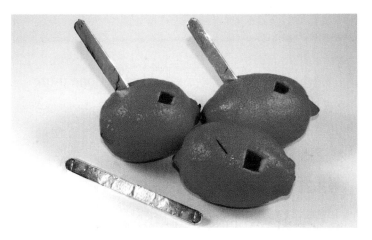

2 Wrap the popsicle sticks with kitchen foil and push one into the slot of each lemon.

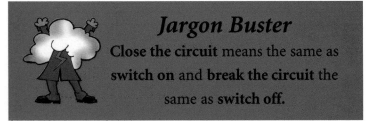

Jargon Buster
Close the circuit means the same as switch on and break the circuit the same as switch off.

3 Push one piece of copper tube into each lemon.

4 Use paper clips to attach the wires.

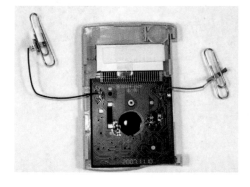

5 You'll need adult help with this step and the next one. Open your calculator to remove the battery and reveal the terminals. This calculator has a red wire marked "+" and a black wire marked "–".

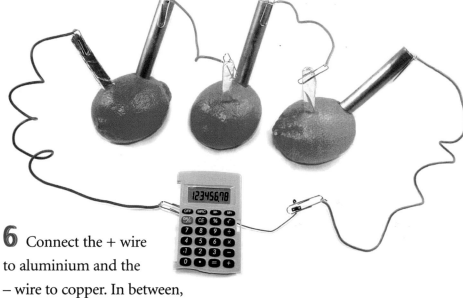

6 Connect the + wire to aluminium and the – wire to copper. In between, make sure copper connects to aluminium.

What's going on?

If we've made all the right connections, after a few minutes we should see the display come on. (If there's a switch, make sure it's on!)

Our lemon battery is producing a charge by having two different metals (aluminum and copper) in an acid liquid (the juice of the lemon). A chemical reaction takes place which also produces an electrical charge. The electricity is conducted through the lemon juice, into the metal, and on into the circuit.

What else can you do?

Try different fruits and vegetables!

Jargon Buster

+ means **positive** —means **negative**
Current in a circuit flows from the terminal marked positive to the one marked negative.

Warning: this page is alarmed!

Now we know how to make a circuit with a battery, lamp, and switch, it's time to put our knowledge to good use!

35 minutes

The plan

We are going to make a simple alarm system. It's meant to be operated by an intruder stepping on a special switch, called a pressure mat.

You will need:

- two sheets of thin card roughly 10 x 8 inches, bigger if you like
- two sheets of kitchen foil—the same area as the cardboard
- thin sponge sheet (sold in craft shops)
- two paper clips
- two long pieces of wire, with stripped ends
- the circuit from page 113
- glue stick, universal glue
- small buzzer (from a hardware store)

What to do:

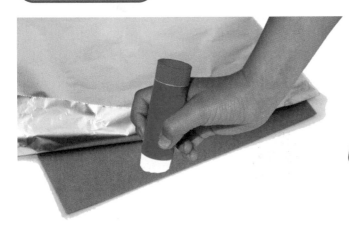

1 Stick foil to both sheets of card.

2 Cut the sponge into strips ½ inch wide.

3 Stick the sponge strips on one foil-covered sheet with a glue stick.

4 Put a paper clip on the edge of the foil. Attach a long wire to the paper clip.

5 Put a paper clip with a long wire on the other sheet.

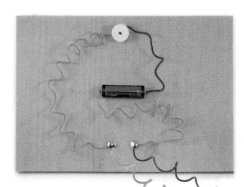

6 Use sticky tape to join the two sheets together, foil side inward. Make sure the paper clips and bare wires can't touch accidentally. This is your new switch.

7 Remove the paper clip from the circuit and connect your new switch to the drawing pins. Replace the lamp with a buzzer.

8 We've put the new switch under a mat.

Buuzzzzzz zzzz...

What's going on?

The weight of someone treading on the pad will complete the circuit and set off the alarm.

What else can you do?

You can make a similar switch that closes when a weight is taken off it.

Attractive stuff

15 minutes

There's a close connection between electricity and another natural force—magnetism. Before we find out more about this connection, we need to look at *magnets*— what they are and how they are made.

You will need:

- at least one magnet— or as many kinds of magnet as you can get
- some objects to test for magnetism, including some made of metal
- a hammer and a piece of scrap wood

The plan

We're going to find out more about the force of magnetism and what it can do.

Experiment 1

1 Take a magnet and hold it near various objects. Which objects are attracted to it?

2 The objects on the right are attracted to the magnet, those on the left are not.

Jargon Buster

A **permanent** magnet means one that does not lose its magnetism.

3 It seems that all the things that the magnet will pick up are metal. But not all metal things are magnetic. Try the magnet with some kitchen foil (aluminum).

What's going on?

All things that are magnetic contain iron. So, for example, steel can be attracted by a magnet, because steel is made of iron mixed with other elements.

Experiment 2

You can use a magnet to make a new one.

1 Take a nail and stroke it lengthwise with one end of the magnet, lifting it away at the end, always using the same end of the magnet.

2 The new magnet won't be as strong as the one that made it, but it can still pick things up!

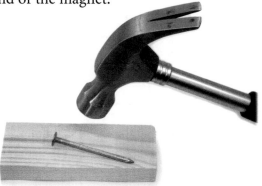

3 Put the magnetized nail on a firm surface and tap it with a hammer along its length. Try not to bend it!

4 We have destroyed the magnetism in the nail.

What's going on?

Nails are made of iron in which the *molecules* are like little magnets arranged randomly. The effect of all the little magnets is to cancel out each other's magnetism. A magnet works because its molecules are all pointing the same way. Stroking a piece of iron (the nail) with a magnet gradually lines up the molecules, magnetizing it.

Hitting the nail with a hammer jars the molecules back into their random arrangement, destroying the magnetic effect.

Magnetic games

30 minutes

Let's look a little more closely at what magnetism can do.

The plan

We are going to look at the ability of magnetism to pass through materials.

You will need:

- two magnets
- marker pen
- a sheet of thin A4 card (8¼ x 11¾ inches)
- two paper clips (different colors would be best)
- a plain glass jar with a plastic lid, clear sides, and no labels
- paper, colored pencils or markers, scissors, sticky tape
- a clean, flat cookie sheet (check that a magnet will stick to it)

Experiment 1

1 Copy the maze onto A4 size card. You and a friend will each need a magnet and paper clip.

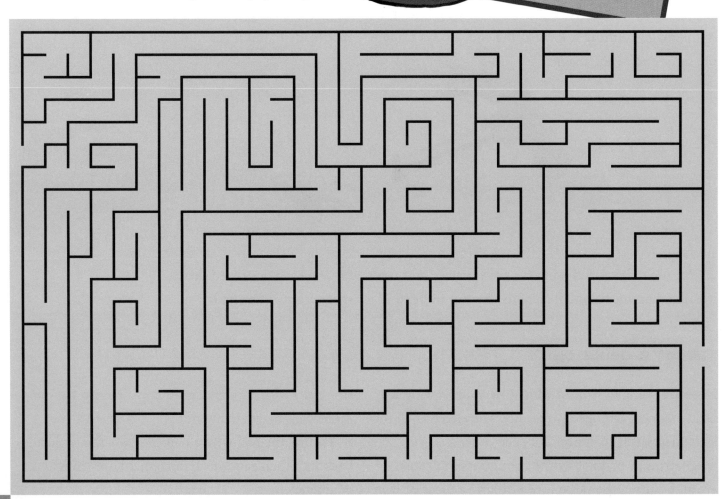

2 Starting at opposite ends, you each guide your paper clip through the maze using magnets under the card. Each of you chooses an entrance and aims for the exit on the other side.

When you've finished, try playing the game again, but this time with the card on a metal cookie sheet. Will the game still work?

Experiment 2

1 Do the Magic Snake trick and baffle your friends! Copy the snake onto paper. Make it a little smaller if necessary, so that it fits in the bottom of the glass jar. Color and cut out the snake.

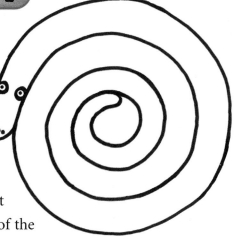

2 Put a paper clip on the snake's head.

3 Stick the tip of the tail to the bottom of the jar.

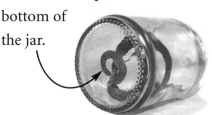

4 Secretly hold a magnet in the palm of your hand as you gently turn the jar upside down and back again.

5 The snake stays up!

6 Take your hand away (with the magnet) and the snake falls down.

What's going on?

In Experiment 1, magnetism passes through the card easily, but not through metal.

In Experiment 2, the snake trick reminds us that just because we can't see something (magnetism), it doesn't mean there's nothing there.

Jargon Buster
A **magnetic field** is the space around a magnet in which magnetism can be detected.

The magnetic Earth

35 minutes

A magnet has a north *pole* and a south pole and so does the Earth. What's the connection?

The plan
We are going to experiment with some magnets and a simple compass.

Experiment 1

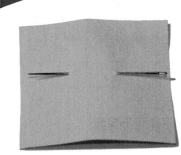

1 Magnetize a needle like the nail on page 121.

2 Thread it through some paper, like this.

What's going on?

Inside the Earth there are massive amounts of iron. It's a huge magnet and our very small needle magnet is responding to it.

Jargon Buster
A **bar magnet** is a straight magnet with the poles at the ends.

3 Float it in a glass of water.

4 The needle will turn round until it settles, pointing north.

Experiment 2

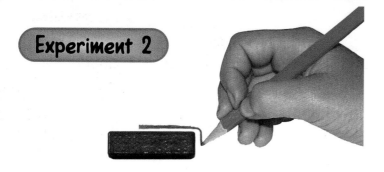

1 Put a magnet on some paper and draw round it so that you can replace it if it gets moved out of position.

2 Move a compass around the magnet in small steps. Draw arrows in each position to show the direction of the compass needle.

3 Continue drawing arrows all around the magnet.

4 The arrows are beginning to form a pattern.

What's going on?

You've drawn a map of a magnetic field! The magnetic field round the Earth is very similar.

5 Join up the little arrows to make curved lines.

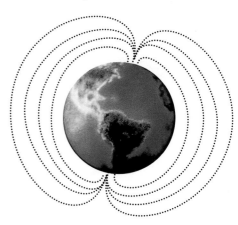

Glossary

Accelerate	Increase velocity.
Alkali	Substance that forms a chemical salt when combined with an acid.
Alkaline	Describes a compound that contains an alkali.
Atom	Smallest particle that makes up a chemical element.
Bacteria	A large group of single cell microorganisms, some of which cause diseases.
Balance	Method used to compare the weights of objects.
Celsius	Scale of temperature measurement most commonly used in science.
Chlorophyll	Chemical that green plants use to help make their food.
Circuit	An electrical circuit is a closed loop, with electricity flowing round it.
Circumference	The distance around a circle.
Compass	An instrument for finding directions on the Earth. It consists of a magnetized pointer which always points north.
Compost	Decayed organic material used as a fertilizer for growing plants.
Conduction	Heat moving from a hotter part of a solid to a cooler part.
Convection	The movement of heat through a liquid or gas caused by hot material rising.
Cycle	A series of events that repeat themselves in the same order.
Density	Degree of compactness of a substance.
Developing	Growing and becoming larger or more advanced.
Displace	Take the place of something.
Echo	A sound caused by the reflection of sound waves from a surface back to the listener.
Evaporate	Turn from liquid into vapor.
Fahrenheit	Scale of temperature measurement commonly used in the United States of America.
Fungi	Spore-producing organisms which feed on organic matter.
Hero's Engine	Invented by Hero of Alexandria in about 62 AD, a heated tank which spins by shooting steam from one or more openings.
Identical	Exactly alike, the same as.
Illusion	An unreal image or impression, a false idea.
Inertia	The way matter continues in its existing state, unless changed by an external force.
Iron filings	Iron filings are very small pieces of iron that look like a dark powder. They are sometimes used in magnetism demonstrations to show a magnetic field.

Kinetic energy	Energy which a body possesses while it's moving.
LCD	Stands for liquid crystal display, a way of displaying shapes, numbers, or letters by applying a current to liquid crystals.
Lens	A piece of glass with one or both sides curved for concentrating or dispersing light rays.
Lift	Upward pressure on an aircraft wing caused by forward motion.
Magnet	A material or object that produces a magnetic field.
Magnetism	A way that a material attracts or repulses another material.
Margarine	Spread used instead of butter, made from vegetable oils and animal fats.
Mass	A measure of the amount of matter in something.
MES	Stands for miniature Edison screw and relates to a light bulb fitting. It is named after Thomas Edison, the inventor.
Neutral	In chemistry, a neutral solution is neither acidic nor alkaline.
Nutrients	Substances that provide food needed for life and growth.
Observation	Statement about what you have learned by using your senses, e.g., heard or seen.
Periscope	A tube or box containing mirrors, designed to increase vision in submarines.
Pigment	A material that changes the color of light it reflects.
Pole	The end of a magnet, north or south, where its magnetic force is strongest.
Potential energy	Energy in an object, such as heat in hot water or tension in a stretched balloon.
Propulsion	Action of driving or pushing forward.
Radiation	A form of energy traveling as rays or waves. Radiation can travel through a vacuum.
Sustained	Something kept going over time.
Smoke	Tiny particles, mostly carbon, distributed through the air.
Temperature	The degree or intensity of heat present in a substance.
Thriving	Doing well, developing correctly.
Transplant	Move to another place or situation or replant a plant.
Velocity	Speed of something in a particular direction.
Virtual	Not really existing as a solid object, appearing as an image or reflection.
Volume	Space occupied by a substance or object, or within a container.

Index

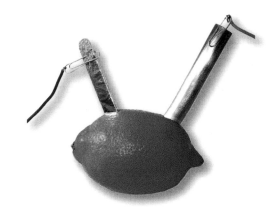

Websites

http://kids-science-experiments.com
http://pbskids.org/zoom/activities/sci
http://sciencemadesimple.com
http://wow.osu.edu/experiments.php
http://www.sciencekidsathome.com
http://www.abc.net.au/spark/experiments/list.htm
http://kids.nationalgeographic.com/Activities/FunScience